Discussion
Booklet IV

**TO LIVE
IS
CHRIST**

TO LIVE IS CHRIST • Discussion Booklet IV •
The Emerging Church: Part 1

FULLY AWARE of religious education as a key factor affecting human relations, the editors invited a Protestant and a Jewish scholar to review material presented in this book as it bears on their respective faith communities. These are Dr. Edward Zerin, Rabbi, who consulted with the American Jewish Committee and Dr. Martin E. Marty, Associate Editor, *Christian Century*. While their personal views and religious beliefs obviously must differ from some of the views presented here, both feel that the content has been so handled as to increase intergroup understanding. While it is hoped that these distinguished authorities similarly will review forthcoming volumes in this series, new materials in preparation will have to await such response at a future date.

the EMERGING church

PART ONE

William J. Kalt *and* Ronald J. Wilkins
with the special assistance of
Dr. Raymond Schmandt

HENRY REGNERY COMPANY  Chicago

NIHIL OBSTAT: Reverend Edward C. Dufficy
Censor Librorum

IMPRIMATUR: Rt. Rev. Msgr. Francis W. Byrne
Vicar General, Archdiocese of Chicago

DATE: *June 5, 1968*

The Nihil Obstat and Imprimatur are official declarations that a book or pamphlet is free of doctrinal or moral error. No implication is contained therein that those who have granted the Nihil Obstat and Imprimatur agree with the contents, opinions, or statements expressed.

The authors assume full responsibility for the final form and content of the text.

Passages from Sacred Scripture contained in the text have been rendered into English accommodated to adolescent comprehension by Father Brendan McGrath, OSB, and the authors.

CONTENTS

Part One

I: FAITH: THE RESPONSE TO GOD IN HISTORY

II: JESUS: THE FOCUS OF HISTORY

III: CHRISTIANITY: THE EMERGING SOCIAL EXPRESSION OF CHRIST IN HISTORY

Part Two

IV: APPENDIX

FAITH:
THE RESPONSE
TO GOD
IN HISTORY

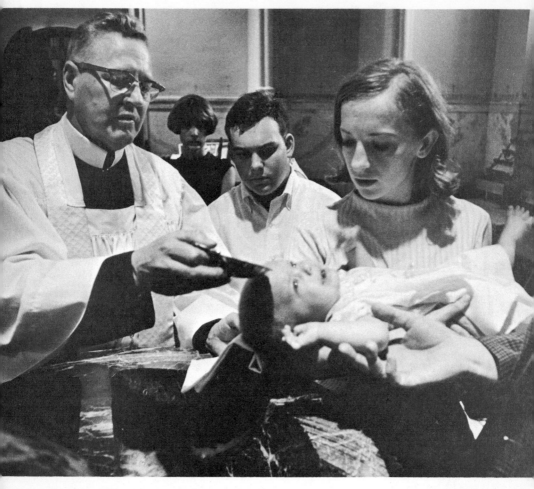

ORLANDO CABANBAN

A questioning Church

You call yourself a Roman Catholic.

Why?

If you are like most people of any religious persuasion you are a Roman Catholic because you were born into a Catholic family. You had no choice in the matter any more than you had a choice of being an American, or white, or Negro, or yellow or red.

Now that you are really old enough to think for yourself, however, you do have a choice, and whether you realize it or not at this moment, your choice is serious. It does make a difference what you believe and how you believe, because your choice affects your actions, attitudes, loves and fears, smiles and tears. This is the most serious question facing you at the moment.

Thoughtful people have always sought an answer to the mystery of life. Their answers have generally led them to the realization that there is more to life than just living. There are so many questions that man finds unanswered even with the advance of science (what is life, really? how do you explain the evil and suffering that people experience? why aren't people able to live in peace and harmony? what lies ahead for people after death? and so on), and yet cannot or will not ignore, that he finds himself respecting mystery though he despises ignorance. Most men have come to the conclusion that there is an answer to life's mystery and that the answer lies outside the individual or society, that it lies outside of man. They have concluded that there is not only an answer, but that there is The Answer and that somehow, sometime, The Answer will be known to man.

3

We Christians believe we have an answer to the mystery of life that makes us unique among all believers in an Ultimate Answer. Roman Catholic Christians believe that our expression of Christianity is historically and theologically more believable than other Christian expressions, not because we look down on other expressions as basically untrue or insincere, but because we find the Roman Catholic expression of the Christian faith more adequate.

Up to this time you may have gone through the motions of being a Catholic. You may have followed the practices of Roman Catholicism without really giving too much thought to why you have done so. Many Catholics your age have had serious doubts about the whole matter, but perhaps you have gone along with your past manner of living your Catholic life because it just was not worth your trouble to do anything else. But now you are at the crossroads of life. The honest decisions you make about the future course of your life will determine to a large extent how you will live your life economically, politically and culturally. If you understand religion to be a celebration of life's ultimate vision, then your religion will be at the very center of your life.

To help you make a decision about your future as a religious person, we invite you to discuss your Roman Catholic faith frankly, intelligently and with an open mind. To do so, you must know what it is, how it expresses itself in the present, and how it will probably express itself in the future.

To know what it is, you must know what it has been. You must know what are the origins of your faith, what Christians thought themselves to be in the past, and what Christians think of themselves now in attempting to move into the future as a living, dynamic group of believers.

To assist you in your discussions, the material in *The Emerging Church* is divided into four parts. The first deals with the phenomenon of *faith* as it is experienced in the lives of most people and with the phenomenon of religious faith as Christians express it. The second deals with the man *Jesus* as he is remembered in the Gospels and in the tradition of the primitive Church. The third part deals with the *Catholic Christian Church* as it understood itself and expressed this understanding culturally in the major historical eras of civilization since its beginnings in Jewish history. Part four is a special *appendix* containing discus-

4

sion material on the Catholic Church in America, the Church of the future, and the general developments of liturgy.

Today the entire Christian Church is trying to understand itself anew. Protestant, Catholic and Orthodox Christians are examining many of their time-honored beliefs and practices to see if they truly express the meaning of Jesus for people on the threshold of transcivilization. Catholic Christians are especially involved in this re-examination, for the momentous decisions of the Second Vatican Council forced Catholics to come to grips with their professed beliefs and practices. In this uncertain age of transition from old ideas to new ideas, every member of the Church from the Pope to your younger brothers and sisters is going through some degree of agonizing re-appraisal about just what it means to be a member of the Catholic Christian Church.

This is not a new experience for the historical Church. Every age of history has caused thinking Christians to try to understand what it means to be a Christian as history moves toward some kind of climax. When a partial answer has been arrived at, Christianity tends to become somewhat stabilized until new social realities move Christians to examine their faith in the light of more advanced theory and practice. During any time of struggle to arrive at a new understanding, there is a period of uncertainty and confusion during which Christians are torn between the "certainties" with which they used to live and the "uncertainties" into which the Christian Church is moving. Such times are always difficult, but they should not be discouraging, for people are moving in the area of faith as they are moving in other areas of life. Like life itself, faith is dynamic; it grows, becomes more mature, and understands itself better.

The elements of
our community faith

As Catholic Christians try to arrive at a truly contemporary understanding of the meaning of Jesus, they are discovering that part of the problem is confusion in the use of terms. Our use of the word "church" is of special concern here.

Sometimes we use the word "church" to describe a *building* where worship takes place. Sometimes we use it to describe an *entire group of people* practicing a certain form of religion, such as the Lutheran Church, the Orthodox Church, the Catholic Church. (Strangely, too, there are groups of people practicing a certain form of religion whom we do not refer to as a "church"; thus, we speak of the Jewish "way of life," the Hindu "religion," the Buddhist "persuasion," and so on.)

Often too, when we are using the term with reference to Roman Catholicism, we use it to designate only its *administrative officers,* for example, when we use such phrases as "The Church teaches . . ." or "The Church says . . ." and so on. This particular narrow usage of the word "church" in Roman Catholic vocabulary has created a problem. Many people do not think of *themselves* as the Church, but only of the "professionals" within the Church as the Church. They think of themselves as some kind of bystanders, outside the mainstream of the Catholic Christian Church.

In this booklet we are using the term "Church" as referring to the entire Catholic community of Christians. We understand the Church to be the community based on Christian **faith.** Our definition of the Church as a faith-community contains *five basic elements:*

1. Our Church is a **community.**
2. It is a community of **faith.**
3. It is a community of faith in **God.**
4. It is a community of faith in a **Saving** God.
5. It is the community of faith in a God who saves **through the man Jesus.**

The first four elements will be explained in this chapter (2). The fifth element will be explained in Chapters 3 and 4. Then, in the remaining six chapters, we will show how the Church throughout history has tried to live out this understanding of what life is all about.

Community

We understand ourselves to be a community of Christians. The word "community" is important. It is intended to be a happy medium between two extremes: the extreme of being some kind of loosely collected club, and the extreme of being a regiment of non-thinking conformists.

We do not form the Church as a loose club of individualists who express our religious feelings in any way we want, who think that whatever pops into our heads is right, who do whatever our impulses suggest. On the other hand, we do not wait for the Church to form us as a passive mass without creative intelligence or personal feelings, thinking only in official categories and doing only what we are told.

We understand our Church to be the medium between these two extremes, a *unified body* with spontaneity as proof of its vitality and unity as a symbol of its meaningfulness. The members of a body live in unity but not uniformity. A body has different kinds of members with different functions. Each performs its own function freely in its own way, but all the members function together for the common good of the body as an integral unit.

This common good is the life of faith.

7

Faith

Like the word "church," the word "faith" has many popular meanings. It is often interchanged with the word "belief." Everyone believes something, everyone has faith in something. An athlete "believes" he can win; a wife has "faith" in her husband; a lover "believes" his beloved will be "faithful"; a dark, cloudy, threatening day leads us to "believe" it will rain; a tornado warning over the radio leads us to "believe" someone has seen a funnel cloud. Not all these beliefs or faiths are equally strong; some may be based on solid reasons, others may be medium or weak because they are based on shaky foundations. Yet, in one way or another, "belief" and "faith" are universal facts of life.

Let us look at *four elements* of "faith" in general which also fit our Christian faith:

1. Faith implies **belief**—a form of *knowing*.
2. Faith implies **trust**—a form of *hoping*.
3. Faith implies **fidelity**—a form of *loving*.
4. Faith implies **free decision**—a form of *risking one's being*.

We will first explain these four elements of any *act* of faith. Then we will discuss the *object* of our religious faith, God.

When we say faith implies *belief,* we mean that faith makes possible an *indirect form of knowledge: a knowing beyond knowing.* I don't "believe" I have two hands if I can see my two hands in front of my face. But I "believe" my hands are connected by nerve cells to my brain because, although I have never seen the nerves inside my hand and never examined my own brain, I believe the statements of scientists who say they have examined the human anatomy from the inside. The athlete doesn't "believe" he won his last competition—he *knows* that; but he believes he can win the next one. The lover doesn't "believe" his beloved is lovable—he directly experiences that; but he believes she is the one he can love best.

Our Christian community belief is a form of knowing which enables the Christian to accept what is beyond man with all it implies. We then believe things we have not experienced directly; and in St. Paul's words faith itself becomes "the substance of things unseen."

When we say faith implies *trust,* we are getting at something deeper than knowledge; we are getting at the personal motivation

UNITED PRESS

LICK OBSERVATORY

DANGER
CONSTRUCTION
AHEAD
PROCEED WITH CAUTION
NEW YORK STATE DEPT. PUBLIC WORKS
SLOW
ONE
LANE

WIDE WORLD

ARMSTRONG ROBERTS

for knowledge. Belief gives us a knowing beyond knowing; this is possible because we *trust* beyond what we directly know.

There are three forms of trust: trust in oneself, trust in other persons, and trust in reality generally. All three forms of trust are implied by faith.

In order to believe anything, we must first of all trust ourselves. We need confidence in our past experience as a basis for what we expect from the future. I believe what I have been told about nerve cells I have never seen because I trust my own experience of being able to move my fingers in response to an idea. An athlete believes he can win the next competition because he trusts his own skill. The lover believes his beloved is the one he can love best because he trusts his judgment in selecting someone for his love.

Faith includes trusting other persons as well as trusting ourselves. Although we know that some people will betray our trust some of the time, we are still willing to trust ordinary people in ordinary situations and to trust better-than-ordinary people in more-than-ordinary situations. I believe what I have been told about my own biological makeup because I trust the research of the scientific community. The athlete believes he can win because he trusts his opponents will compete fairly and the referees will judge fairly. The lover trusts his beloved to accept his love and to love him in return.

Trust in ourselves and others is grounded in a basic trust in reality. Even though evil and betrayal exist in the world, we sense that these are human fallings away from a deeper reality of goodness and fidelity. And we sense that human evil is never perfectly malicious and that human betrayal is not the constant state of mankind. The basis for our ordinary trust of human beings by-and-large is our sense that most people want to face reality most of the time—that the real world is finally the only one worth living in.

In the case of our Christian faith, we believe the things we do because we trust ourselves, we trust others, and we trust reality. We trust ourselves to be able to make a mature judgment about life and what it means; we trust others (such as the apostles, the writers of Scripture, the teaching authorities of the Church) to be sincere and objective in their account of what we believe; and we trust reality to be capable of inspiring such trustworthiness.

When we say faith implies *fidelity,* we are moving from the area of receiving to the area of giving. The first two elements of faith (believing and trusting) are acts by which we receive something: we accept as "true" a form of *knowledge* beyond our direct experience, and we accept others in what they present to us as "true." But now *we* must somehow be "true" to what we have received. We are true to what we have received if we give witness to it as part of reality in our lives and words, because, if we accept this knowing beyond knowing as true, it will make a difference in what we say and do. We will share our knowledge with others so that by their believing us their own mental horizons might be enlarged; and we will wish to be trustworthy so that they can be secure in their trust of us.

We speak of "keeping faith" with other persons, of being "faithful" to our promises. This fidelity is an aspect of Christian faith. Our beliefs make demands on us, to which we promise to be faithful. Our fellow Christians expect this fidelity from us in the name of Him to whom we owe everything.

The fourth element of faith is *free decision.* Belief and trust and fidelity are not things which can be forced. They demand a kind of "leap," an abandonment of security. Partial knowledge is the basis for believing what we do not completely know. Partial experience is the basis for trusting persons and events we cannot completely control. Partial fulfillment is the basis for being faithful to demands we cannot completely foresee in advance. A scientist's belief in some biological theory is based on his partial experiments and his decision about the validity of the reports of fellow scientists on countless other experiments. An athlete's belief that he can win depends on his decision about the kind of opponent he is facing and the fairness of the judges, as well as on the reliability of the conditions under which he will be competing. A lover's belief that his beloved is faithful is a decision based on what can never be absolutely proved but is an extension of the partial experience he has had of his beloved's love. A lover's promise of fidelity is a free decision to risk his happiness upon the one human being he has chosen to receive the gift of himself.

This leap of faith—of believing, trusting, being faithful— is an act of risking one's whole being, one's whole way of life, upon something outside oneself, something one cannot completely understand or control or secure in advance.

11

When we say The Church is a community of faith, we mean that we are a group of people who have freely decided to risk our lives in such a leap. We believe, we trust, we promise fidelity to something very basic about life—something we cannot directly prove or experience, but which nevertheless seems worthy of our life-commitment because our common experience of life makes sense in terms of this commitment. This decision should not be something we have been "brainwashed" into, something we accept simply because we were born into it, or something we decide because we want to conform and drift with the crowd. The faith which binds us together as a Church is not a true faith for us, unless we personally have decided that our community's interpretation of life is something we personally believe, trust, and commit ourselves to.

What are the results of making this decision to believe? Once we have freely decided to believe, we establish a frame of reference for our lives—a basic philosophy by which we direct our lives. Such a decision frees us from anxiety, sets guidelines for our actions, enables us to understand the human limitations of our own and others' beliefs, and provides for growth and understanding of our own relationships with the One who is trusted.

What precisely is the object of this free decision to believe, trust, and commit ourselves? We call it God. We have described our Church as a community of faith. It is not a community of faith in anything and everything. It has a specific faith, faith in God. This faith in God, like any faith, has four elements: belief in God, trust in God, fidelity to God, free decision about God.

God

What is "God"?

This question has burned in men's minds for centuries. It is too big to be settled in one book, certainly too big for this booklet whose purpose is not to focus on "God" as such but on "Church history." (A companion volume to this booklet, *The Religions of Man,* gives more detail on mankind's various conceptions of God.) Here we will summarize *four basic elements* of the Christian notion of "God." These four elements are not original with Christianity, but they are very sharp and clear in Christianity:

1. The basis of Reality is **Totally Other.**
2. The Absolute Other **makes sense.**
3. The Absolute Other is **Personal.**
4. The Absolute Other is **One.**

When we say that the basis of Reality is *Totally Other,* we are talking about an experience of life that is not a once-and-for-all insight. It is a kind of basic wisdom about life that we learn more and more deeply as life goes on.

Our first suspicion of the "Otherness" of Reality comes to us when we learn that we are not going to get everything we want in life. Our first instinct is to think there is something wrong with Reality because it is not centered around ourselves personally. But as we get older, the true character of Reality begins to hit home to us. Life's hard knocks accumulate. We begin to learn that Reality ultimately operates on a principle that is "Not-me." Reality is Other than me. In fact, Reality is quite free of me. Anything I have could be taken away, stolen, lost, burned, killed, or destroyed. Even *I* could be taken away from myself—I could be hurt in an accident and lose a limb, lose my memory, lose my mind, lose my life. I am totally dependent upon whatever Reality gives me.

This Totally Other quality of Reality hits me not only in life's hard knocks but in the good times as well. Perhaps the most shattering experience of life is not what goes *wrong,* but the realization that even what goes *right* is something I do not have absolute claim upon. My best thoughts "come" to me; my best friend "gives" his fidelity to me; my best talents "happen" to be part of me. What makes me me is fundamentally not me.

When this Not-me character of Reality has really hit home to a person, he is faced with a decision—either all of this is absurd or else it is all a gift. Either it *makes sense* that I should be from and for and in what is not-me, or else life is nonsense.

Do I dare trust Reality? Something so all-powerful that I have no control over it whatsoever unless It gives me some kind of partial control? Does Reality make any sense at all?

Some persons say no. There are those who reject Reality and prefer to live in a dream world of their own making rather than trust themselves to the real world upon which they depend.

13

There are others who have decided they will live in the real world, even though its basic principle of operation is Something Other than themselves. Living in the real world means living in a world that is not centered around me. It means living a life that is not centered around me. It means Something Right is at the bottom of everything that happens—Something bigger than I am—Something so important that I can live for It and die for It, and both my life and my death will make sense as long as I am living or dying for *It*.

Why should I trust myself to an "It"?

There are many people in the world whose basic religious belief is in an Impersonal Force, a Fundamental Power of the Universe, or just plain Matter itself.

There are others, including those in the Catholic Christian Church, who have decided to believe (to accept as true) that something so trustworthy, so free of control by men, must be *Personal*. Those whose religious belief takes the form of belief in a Personal God explain themselves this way: *if Reality can produce persons, how could Reality Itself be something less than the persons It produces?*

Believing that the Absolute Other is Personal adds a new warmth to the basic act of trust that we place in *It*. Instead of merely "resigning ourselves to an Impersonal Reality" we can "give ourselves to God." Christians and other theists* believe in a Personal God who can be trusted. Christians do not claim they can *prove* that God is trustworthy; no trust can be proved. If any trust could be proved, it would not be an act of trust but an act of complete knowledge. Believers in the Christian God are those who have *decided* to trust on the basis of partial experience.

Just as the athlete cannot prove he can win, and a wife can never have absolute proof her husband will be faithful, so the believer in God cannot "prove" that life makes sense or that God will do what is best.

One difference between the wife's faith in her husband and the religious believer's faith in God is that the wife trusts someone who is only a part of reality while the religious believer trusts The One who is the basis of All of Reality.

The wife's trust in her husband can never be absolute, for he might one day refuse to live up to reality; but the Christian

---

* From the Greek word *Theos,* meaning "God."

trusts God absolutely, for Reality can never refuse to live up to Itself.

It is this absolute trust in Reality which helps explain our religious ancestors' gradual growth away from belief in many gods to belief in *One God*. If we trust that Reality ultimately makes sense, this implies that there cannot be many Ultimate Realities at variance with one another; there must be ultimately One Explanation of our life and death.

In capsule form, this is what we mean by speaking of our Church as a community of faith in God. *We are those who have decided to join together to celebrate our belief that life makes sense*. We celebrate it with one another and with The One who calls us into being today. We trust The One, and we trust one another because we know that we are expressions of The One. As personal fragments of reality, we join together in the celebration of life which is One Reality.

God Saves

We have been building the Christian definition of the Church element by element. We have arrived at the point where we see that our Church is a community of those who believe that Reality is ultimately Personal. But that is not enough. Many communities believe this much. The Jewish and Christian communities have still more elements to add.

It is not enough to know that at its very source, Reality has a Personal attitude toward us. We must still ask: what kind of Personal attitude?

There are three possible answers: either God is hostile to man; or God is indifferent; or God is friendly.

Many primitive religions have assumed that God is hostile; in their eyes, Reality is against us, toying with us, unfriendly. Some primitive men thought they had to "buy God off" by offering human sacrifices to satisfy his thirst for human blood. Or they tried to trick God into doing what they wanted by forcing his hand through magic rites which they thought gave them power over God. Or they tried to fool God by pretending to be what they were not. All these attitudes assume that God is not on our side to begin with.

Some other religions have not assumed that God is hostile, but they have not assumed he is friendly either; they have pictured him as being neutral, indifferent, basically unconcerned about man. In poetic language we might picture their God as winding up the universe and then leaving it alone to tick itself off in its own direction. Such a view can interpret life as an eternal cycle beginning nowhere, ending nowhere. Men might feel they are mere cogs in the universal machine, cranking away until some day they die and are replaced by new cogs—all without purpose, meaning or future.

In contrast to these two views, we and our Jewish brothers have inherited from our common Jewish ancestors a more hopeful view of God's Personal attitude towards us. We believe that God is man's Friend, that He is concerned about us, that His concern is as real as the concern of our human friends. Because we believe that God is man's Friend, our belief contains *four elements,* conclusions from our experience with God which have shaped our history and brought us to where we are today:

1. God is **man's Partner** in man's history.
2. God saves His people **from** some misfortunes.
3. God saves us **through** all misfortunes always.
4. God directs history to a **climax.**

These four elements are our way of saying "God saves."

We believe this *now,* because we believe it happened in the past. We trust that God will save us finally, because He has saved our ancestors in the past. We have no "proof" that He will thus save us; we *believe* that He will do so because He is a Personal God who has acted in our history. We trust that He will continue to do so.

Our trust in God is based upon our history. The record of that history begins with what we call the Old Testament. Briefly it goes like this.

Our Judeo-Christian interpretation of history begins, as you know, with the call of **Abraham** and his clan around 1900 B.C. to leave the Mesopotamian system of many nature-gods and with their Covenant to be faithful to only One God no matter where they wandered.

From these pre-Jewish roots, Hebrew religion survived and grew until the time of the Exodus from Egypt about 1285 B.C. when **Moses** and his people swore a Covenant in the desert with

16

Yahweh* as their National God.** They were God's *People;* He was *their* God. God and man were partners. A community of believers was born, not by human invention but by divine intervention.

After arriving in Canaan, which in later times was called Palestine and today is called Israel, the descendents of these people continued to grow in deeper knowledge of God and His ways of dealing with men. We remember the **prophets** and their specially inspired preaching which led the people to take their Covenant with God more and more seriously.

The first point to notice in this familiar history is the tremendous conviction this people had that Yahweh had sworn a Covenant of friendship and partnership with them. They were sure that they were a *chosen* people. They believed that God wanted to do something good in the world through them.

This belief in their Covenant with God arose directly out of their experience. For more than 3200 years, the Jewish people have constantly looked back upon the Exodus as the wondrous sign that God intends to *save them* for the sake of all mankind. Many slaves had died in Egypt; only a few escaped. Why did the Hebrew group succeed in their escape and many others not?

Their answer lies in the very nature of the Jewish idea of Covenant. They believed that Yahweh was a God *of the people,* of the entire clan, and not a God of an individual Jew who would save him and not the rest of the community. They believed this also because they believed that Yahweh acted *in their experience of life* (which He had given them) and not in some other world or life outside of their experience. They believed that Yahweh would save them in their life as a people, a community of believers. Finally they believed that this saving of them as a people was an ongoing process—it would finally happen, no matter what happened to individuals. And this belief was justified, for it really did happen. Because they believed, they trusted Yahweh. Because their trust was honored, they believe that their God is a saving God—a God who saves his people.

While we do not see the entire Plan of God in all its details, we can certainly see in retrospect that this people who escaped from Egypt set mankind on a spiritual journey up and

---

* This is the Hebrew name for the Hebrew God, meaning "He who Is" or "He who causes to be."
** *Exodus* 19:3-7.

17

away from slavery to new heights of love for their fellow men. As slaves, they had learned a lesson: slavery is inhuman. When they arrived in their "promised land," they made laws which were the most human in their part of the world. Though they did not abolish slavery entirely, they drastically limited it, even requiring that in their own land slaves should be set free every seven years. Their basic attitude was so humanitarian that it became possible for mankind's conscience to evolve in sensitivity to the point where today slavery is virtually unknown in those parts of the world where the Jewish religion (and its offspring Christianity) is lived up to.

Looking back with the Jewish people on their history, we can see with them that the Exodus was not an accident. We can perceive it as a Word from God saying, "I am with you, working in and through you. As individuals you will live and die, but the world will be better because you have lived and died. This I promise you. And while your mind is not large enough to see *all* the good your life and death are accomplishing, you can't miss seeing some of it—enough to know that I am with you."

The Exodus is an example of God saving us *from* misfortune. But the Jewish people were not spared other misfortunes. Many times throughout the centuries they have been raided, attacked, persecuted, taken captive. Even in modern times the memory of Hitler's slaughter of over six million Jews in Europe is heavy upon the Jewish people and a blot on the conscience of Christians who allowed such a thing to happen in a Christian country. Why does God save man from some misfortunes but not others?

We do not have a final answer to this question, but we can find, as the Jewish people of today do, some glimpse of God's Plan by remembering another great event of some centuries before Christ—**The Babylonian Exile** of 587 B.C. and the return to Palestine in 536 B.C. At the time when the Babylonians attacked Jerusalem, destroyed the Temple, and deported the bulk of the Jewish population to Babylon, everything pointed to the death of the Covenant.

But just the opposite happened—the Covenant between God and his people grew more firm than before. Not only did Yahweh show that He was their saving God by restoring them to their native land, He led the Jews to a better understanding of Him through three important results of their exile. First of all, the exile renewed in Jewish minds the centrality of the Covenant and the importance of their living up to their part. Second, the Jewish people added to their Temple worship a greater study of their Torah* and traditions; out of this study came the massive editing and compiling which created The Bible in the form we recognize as the Old Testament. Third, as a result of the Jews' living so long in Babylon, a knowledge of God's action in Salvation History was spread throughout Babylonian culture. Thus, looking at history through eyes of faith opened by the Jewish awareness of God, we can see that *God is man's partner in moving history forward to a climax.* He uses good and evil, fortune and misfortune, the totality of human experience, to help us achieve a monumental task—the creation of the world to its final and perfected state.

Today, this basic trust that God is working in history is so much a part of us that as Christian believers we can see God's work in many aspects of history which do not appear, on first glance, to be "religious" history at all.

For example, we can look at the commonly accepted facts of prehistoric evolution as telling a marvelous story of the universe; in our mind's eye we can see the passage of millions of prehistoric years as a parade of organic compounds in the ocean becoming one-celled creatures becoming creeping and crawling things becoming amphibians becoming lizards becoming dinosaurs and birds and mammals becoming primates and anthropoids and hominids and finally—Man. The Christian can see in the universe progressively revealing itself and its pattern of overall change the action of God which gave and continually gives man and the world being and meaning.

We do not see the reasons for everything that happened; yet we see in the overall picture enough glimpses of light to believe that everything that happened is intelligible. We do not see Man as a freak, unprepared for by the universe. We see Reality on our side.

But Christians are realists about the obstacles, too. They see that this thrust for creation to move toward and into intelligence is only one phase of the evolutionary process. They believe that creation (having moved into the sphere of intelligence, that

---

* This Hebrew word means both teachings and law, making up a total "way of life."

19

part of creation we call "man") still has a long way to go. We are far from what we *should be* because, like all parts of creation, we are what we *have been*. We retain much of our past as we move to the future. Even though Christian faith is hopeful, it still realizes that the "not yet" is not yet and that mankind has many struggles, many sorrows still facing it. This human condition, the basic inability of man to achieve his ideal in the present, shows its effects in acts of selfishness or self-centered concern, of hurt to others, of lying, stealing, cheating, of prejudice, discrimination, and hate, of civil disorder, of race riots and of war. The Christian Churches take man for what he is: an imperfect creature moving toward perfection. The Christian Churches understand man and his place in God's creative acts. They believe that God made one creature, man, not only capable of knowledge and love, but capable of knowing and loving God in Himself and in what He did in such a way that man's love rises to a plane that makes possible the true mutuality that love demands. It is in this way that they see him as part of a total evolutionary plan, of a history that they call "Salvation History."

Salvation history is thus more than Biblical history; it is an interpretation of *all* history. Faith that "God saves" is an act of trust that God is on man's side even when man cannot see how. It is an act of trust that man and the universe are working together for the good of both, even though we have only the faintest glimpse of what Reality still wants us to become.

The man Jesus

Up to now, our description of the Christian faith in a Saving God has shown, element by element, what we have in common with the Jewish faith from which ours springs. The Jewish faith has continued to evolve and is a vital force in the world today. But our Christian faith adds an element to Salvation History not found in the classic Jewish interpretation of life. That is the element of *focus*—of God's appearance in history focused to complete presence in one man, Jesus of Nazareth.

The importance of Jesus in focusing God's presence in history will be discussed in the next two chapters.

This chart summarizes what we have discussed in the preceding pages and also anticipates what will be discussed in the next unit. It shows how the world's various faiths are related to one another from our Catholic Christian point of view.

JESUS:
THE FOCUS
OF HISTORY

The Saving God in Person

The role of Messiah

In the preceding unit we showed how the faith which forms our Christian community is related to other faiths. It is more than a general faith in life; it is faith in God. It is more than a general faith in an abstract God; it is faith in a Saving God who has introduced Himself to us in history. In this section we summarize our faith that God introduced Himself finally and perfectly in the man *Jesus*,* who fulfilled in his life and person all that his people had been prepared to expect of a Saving God. As we Christians remember him, he fulfilled this expectation in the role of Messiah**—God's Anointed One.

Let us look briefly at what this role meant in Jesus' day. We must begin by drawing a contrast between earlier pagan religion and the developed Jewish religion of his time.

When primitive man explained the source of the threats to his well-being in terms of a spirit world acting for or against him, and began to take means to offset the forces which threatened him, we have the beginnings of what we call primitive religion.† He began to perform those distinctly religious ceremonies which were designed to ward off the anger of his gods or to shield him from hostile spirits bent on his destruction. Whenever he could, he used his own wits and his own power to

---

* The name Jesus (or *Yehoshua*) is a Hebrew word meaning "God saves."
** From the Greek translation of this word, *Christos*, which means "christened" or "anointed," we get the name "Christ."
† See *Religions of Man*, Chapter 2, "Prehistoric religion."

24

overcome his enemies, but he experienced certain forces he could not explain and could not outwit. These forces he tried to overcome by special ceremonies and actions which, he believed, would save him when the spirit world was not pleased with him.

When men began to live together in community, they were united in common efforts to provide the necessities of life and in common worship of spirits that they believed inhabited their world. They selected certain persons in the community to perform their religious acts—and to represent the community to win the favor of the gods or to ward off hostile spirits.

As time went on and civilizations became more sophisticated, so did the practice of religion. But the basic idea was still there and was celebrated in the religious feasts of all early religions by which the gods of the spirit world were honored. Those gods that were favorable received gifts; those that were hostile were bought off, if possible, by sacrifice. Thus, in many cases of religious development in early civilization, man felt the need to be saved from forces of the spirit world.

When Abraham left his Mesopotamian culture and went in search of his God, he retained many of the cultural expressions of religion that had come from his ancestors, but it is evident a new relationship to God was dawning for men. Six hundred years later when his descendants found themselves in slavery in Egypt, they believed that they were delivered from their slavery by their God—the God of Abraham—who, they said, sent Moses to be their leader. So strong was their conviction that they had been saved from this worst of all misfortunes by their God that it became the focal point of their religion and was the central message of their history. Many years later they recounted this saving act in the book telling about their delivery in the following way:

Exodus

20:1 I am Yahweh your God
who brought you out of the land of Egypt,
out of the house of slavery.

Time and again in their books the Jewish people tell how God saved them. No matter what the misfortune, the Jewish people believed that God would save them; they believed he would somehow rescue them from their misfortunes.

You may have noticed a very subtle change in the idea of salvation from some primitive pagan religions to the Hebrew

25

religion. In the former, religious practices were sometimes performed to protect the people *from* the gods. In Judaism, the saving action was performed *by* God. In the more advanced Jewish notion, we see how God was leading man to a better understanding of God himself through their developing self-understanding.

When the Hebrews in the time of Moses accepted salvation through their God as a very part of their history, they realized that *God was saving them through the actions of men,* men who, they believed, were sent by God to carry out his saving actions. For the Jewish people it was all very simple: because God was trustworthy he would send a savior to deliver them as he had always done, if they were faithful to God. If they were not, disaster would strike the entire nation. So it was that the idea of *particular saviors* became a part of the Hebrew religious heritage.

In the early centuries after Moses molded a people in Yahweh's name, various saviors called **judges** arose from time to time to lead the people in military victory over their pagan opponents who had been oppressing them.

The Chosen People became even more unified when the prophet Samuel anointed their very first king, **Saul,** around the year 1020 (to 1000) B.C. The coronation ceremony for the king included pouring sacred oil over his head. Since he was thus anointed, he was called God's anointed one, or Messiah. After Saul came **David,** who ruled from 1000 to 961 B.C. as the greatest Israelite king. He in turn was succeeded by his son **Solomon,** whose two sons plunged the Israelite kingdom into civil war.

The Israelite kingdom never recaptured the splendor and glory of the reign of David. Thus, for centuries he was looked back to as the ideal ruler, the ideal Messiah, the ideal savior-king.

When the Jewish people were deported to Babylon in 587 B.C. and returned to their land in 536 B.C., they longed to restore the powerful kingdom their ancestors had known in the golden days of King David. They looked forward to the day when God would raise up a new Messiah in David's tradition.

By the time Jesus appeared, the idea of savior-Messiah had pretty well solidified into the notion that *soon* God would send someone to restore Israel to its former glory. The Jewish people had been under foreign rule for over 300 years, and, though several Jewish commanders had succeeded for short periods of time in rebellion and had given the Jews a measure of political freedom, none had really succeeded in establishing

26

Judaism in its hoped-for place as the leader of all nations and the instrument for bringing Yahweh's rule to all people.

It is not hard to understand why the Jews expected a Messiah, given their religious history and their way of life, so opposed to the accepted pagan moral and religious practices. It is difficult, however, to understand why Jesus succeeded where others failed. Why should Jesus, who preached an unmilitary, non-political idea of the kingdom of God, have made such an impression on his followers that he was accepted as *The* Messiah to change the course of history? The answer we believe lies in the Christian memory of how the apostles experienced Jesus.

The man who fulfilled the role

What do we know about Jesus? We certainly have no more person-to-person knowledge of him than we do of, say, George Washington or of John F. Kennedy. If the Jesus of history or the Christ of faith is to have any meaning for us here and now, we must reflect on the meaning of Jesus as he is presented by those who knew him and believed that he was the Lord and the Anointed One. This is the role that the **New Testament** plays in the Christian Church: it is the norm of the faith of Christians. Reflection on the New Testament has been the source for the expression of our faith in the past; it will be the source for the expression of our faith in the future.

However, the New Testament is not, as some have mistakenly thought, a biography of Jesus.* It is, rather, a collection of theological sketches *about* Jesus. That is, though we have some facts about Jesus' life (the historical Jesus), what really comes through in the New Testament is not bare facts, but *impact:* what the apostles and first Christians remembered about Jesus *because* they believed him to be the Christ.

There is no doubt in the minds of the apostles or in the reflections of the primitive Christian community that Jesus had the ultimate role in the plan of God. The unique feature of this

---

* There are many biographies of Jesus in print today. They are attempted reconstructions of what probably happened given the details of his life and the findings of archeologists and historians. They are *not* exact biographies.

27

Dali: "Christ of St. John of the Cross"

conviction is that the apostles and early Christians did not experience Jesus as a God in human disguise or as God pretending to be human (this is one reason that the early Church rejected fanciful and wildly imaginative accounts of Jesus' life). *They experienced him as a human.* He was so real in his life, so genuinely human in his spirit, and so convincing in his words that they believed in him. They felt that *whatever human life really was, Jesus as a person expressed that life.*

We get some factual data about Jesus' life from the gospels. But it is frustrating data. We do not know exactly when he was born or when he began his public life. ("In the fifteenth year of the reign of Tiberius,"* does not give us exact dates or at what time of year, what month or what day.) According to our present reckoning, Jesus was born sometime around 4 B.C. and died near the year 30 A.D. We presume that he lived the life of an ordinary Jewish child and adolescent (we have only a glimpse of his pre-adult years in the Temple incident) and experienced the joy and sorrow, triumph and frustration of the average, small town Hebrew male.**

Even the public portion of Jesus' life, about which we know most, is cloudy as far as details are concerned. We are not sure if his public life was one year or three, but we assume it was more than one and perhaps less than three. What we do know for certain is that during his itinerant preaching career (he wandered from his home province of Galilee to the capital in Jerusalem to the wilderness of the Jordan River and the Syrian desert to the towns and villages of Samaria, which lay between Galilee and Judea) a crisis built up that became so severe that Jesus was finally put to death by the Roman authorities at the insistence of some religious leaders among the Jews.

There are several other external facts that we accept, such as his baptism by John in the Jordan, his spending some time alone in a deserted area to sort out his thoughts, his selecting a group of intimate followers, attending a wedding at Cana and

---

* *Luke* 3:1
** It is important for modern-day Christians to remind themselves that Jesus was a Jew. He was born into a Jewish family, raised in a Jewish culture, educated in the ways and in the manner of Jewish boys and followed all the customs and practices of Jewish life. In his preaching and in his teaching Jesus used Jewish thought patterns, manners of expression, and figures of speech.

29

occasionally staying with friends. We suppose he had no permanent home, payed taxes, attended the Jewish festivals and talked to countless numbers of people. But still the details are blurred and uncertain to us. Accustomed as we are to instant communication and exact detail, such uncertainty and carelessness with detail (was his famous sermon on a mountain, on a flat piece of ground, or on a hill? Were there 5000 present or 20,000? Was it 3 or 4 miles out in the lake or halfway across that he calmed the sea?) can be exasperating. But, apparently, details were of so little importance to the apostles and the early writers that they were not concerned with exactness. Evidently *what* Jesus said or *meant* was the important thing, not where or how many were present.

Why was this so? As we have said, the apostles and writers were not writing historical biography (in our sense) or biographical history. *They were concerned with meaning.* Convinced, finally, of who Jesus was and what this meant, they *reconstructed* the life of Jesus to best *bring out the meaning* of this life. For them, three things were important to bring out their point: the **preaching** of Jesus, the **miracles** of Jesus and the **death-resurrection** event. They arranged the chronology to emphasize these three aspects.

The preaching of Jesus

According to primitive Christianity, what *was* the message of Jesus? One evangelist summarizes it in the opening verses of his gospel:

Mark

1:14 Jesus went to Galilee.
There he proclaimed the Good News
of the Kingdom of God:
15 *"The time is ripe,"* he said,
and the kingdom of God is coming close!
Change your heart and mind
and believe the good news!"

This was the essence of Jesus' message.

Jesus' use of this term "kingdom of God," went beyond the popular view of many of his listeners who understood the

30

kingdom in the sense of Judaism finally reigning with power over other nations and occupying a place of power in the political arena. As the Gospels tell it, Jesus did not see the Kingdom of God in terms of territory, rule, sovereignty, armies and submission due to conquest. He saw it as the condition in the world in which all men would accept the idea of God's influence on their lives and would live their lives guided by Jesus' vision of God's plan for the fulfillment of his creation. Jesus understood the kingdom in terms of man's becoming what he was called to be.

But Jesus was no idle visionary. He knew man's sinfulness, his selfish tendencies and his laziness. But he also fathomed his need to be urged to do better things. He directed his preaching to *the most urgent need of mankind:* common justice and decency for those who did not have it.

We can appreciate the excitement that Jesus' preaching created among his hearers when we realize that Jesus was proposing that *the kingdom of God was here on earth, not in some "other" world, not for the privileged members of society, and not to be awarded for fulfilling pietistic rituals.* Jesus' "kingdom of God" was a here and now event.* It included everyone willing to accept the idea of God as Jesus preached it, and it was evident in those who believed by the way they cared for their neighbors.

It was clear to Jesus that as long as there was imposed suffering, poverty and enslavement, as long as the poor, the gentle, the downcast, the deprived, the forgiving, the naive, the retarded, the crippled, the blind and the lame were considered outcasts from polite society, as long as minority groups were the subject of prejudice and discrimination, the kingdom of God was not present. How could God reign as long as injustice was present on earth?

Jesus did not try to solve the mystery of suffering; he urged his followers *to do something about it.* His message was a social message: God's people must show concern for the many who did not enjoy the material benefits of the world. On this, and on this alone, would Christians be judged.

Matthew

25:31 When the Son of Man comes in His majesty . . .

34 The King will say to those on His right hand,

---

* *Luke* 17:21

31

"Come, you who have been blessed by my Father,
and possess the kingdom prepared for you
since the creation of the world.
35 Yes, I was hungry and you fed me;
I was thirsty and you gave me something to drink;
I was a stranger and you made me welcome;
36 I was naked and you gave me clothes;
I was sick and you came to visit me;
I was in jail and you came to see me."
37 Then the righteous will reply to Him,
"Lord, when did we see you hungry and feed you,
or thirsty and give you something to drink?
38 When did we ever welcome you in as a stranger
or see you naked and clothe you?
39 When did we realize you were sick or in prison
and come to visit you?"
40 The King will answer them,
"I tell you the absolute truth:
Whenever you did it
for one of these brothers of mine,
insignificant though he may be,
you were doing it for me."
41 Then He will address those on His left,
"Get out of my presence, you damned ones,
into the eternal fire prepared for the devil and his angels!
42 I was hungry but you wouldn't give me anything to eat;
I was thirsty and you gave me nothing to drink;
43 I was a stranger and you didn't take care of me;
I was naked but you wouldn't give me something to wear;
I was sick and in prison and you didn't come to see me."
44 And they too will ask Him,
"Lord, when did we ever see you hungry or thirsty,
or come upon you as a stranger or naked,
or know that you were sick or in prison,
and not take care of your needs?"
45 And He will answer them,
"Listen to the truth:
If you ever turned your back on anyone as 'insignificant,'
then you were turning your back on me."

That is why Jesus' whole message about the kingdom is summarized in what is called "The Sermon on the Mount." This is not a single sermon preached by Jesus; it was a summary of his entire message. It is put at the beginning of St. Matthew's gospel to show that Jesus' preaching of the kingdom—and its establishment on earth—would make things better for the under-privileged.* In effect, Jesus was saying that in God's kingdom (as opposed to the kingdoms they were used to):

> The poor would be better off.
> The gentle would not be abused.
> The sad would receive sympathy and understanding.
> The people who want to do what is right,
> those who are forgiving,
> the sincere, trustful people,
> those who work for peace,
> and those who are the object of hatred and scorn
> because they work for justice,
> would all be included in the kingdom.

For Jesus the kingdom of God and a society that excluded hatred, violence and revenge, and worked actively for the better-ment of social conditions for the poor and the underprivileged were synonymous. When John the Baptist, the most influential of the prophets of Jesus' time, sent friends to ask Jesus for his credentials as Messiah, Jesus said:

Matthew

> *11:4* Go on back and tell John
> what you hear and see:
> the blind see again,
> the lame walk,
> lepers are cleansed,
> the deaf hear, . . .
> *5* and the Good News is preached
> to the poor.

Jesus stressed that the kingdom of God would be present when all men were brothers, when there was no privilege, no discrimination and no prejudice. Jesus said that, contrary to the accepted notion of the time, everyone was to be included, even one's enemies, when God's kingdom was realized.

---

* See *Matthew* 5, 6, and 7. Also *Luke* 6.

6:27 For you who will listen, I say:
Love your enemies,
do good to those who hate you.

28 Bless those who curse you
and pray for those who tear down your reputation.

29 Show your other cheek to one who slaps your face,
and if someone is taking your coat
don't refuse him your jacket.

32 If you love only those who love you,
how does that make you worth anything?
After all, every sinner loves those who love him.

35 The real thing is to love your enemies,
and to do favors and lend things
without expecting anything for it . . .

36 You should be compassionate,
just as your Father is compassionate.

37 Don't pass judgment
and judgment will not be pronounced against you.
Don't condemn and you will not be condemned.
Forgive and you will be forgiven.

· *45* A good man has good resources
in his heart to draw from;
a bad man can only bring forth bad things
from an evil heart . . .

31 Treat people the same way
you want them to treat you.

Jesus' message of brotherhood was based upon his understanding of the common Fatherhood of God. His entire life was directed toward preaching this reign of God, and his own personal actions bore out his preaching. He sought out the poor and the sick, he "ate with sinners,"* he demonstrated compassion and sympathy for those in trouble, and he identified himself with those whom society excluded.

Jesus' own philosophy of life is neatly expressed in an incident remembered in St. Matthew's gospel:

---

* *Matthew* 9:11, *Mark* 2:15, *Matthew* 11:19, *Luke* 7:34.

22:35 A lawyer once asked him,

36 "Teacher, what is the great commandment of the Torah?"

37 And Jesus answered,

"Love the Lord your God with your whole heart
and your whole soul and your whole mind.

38 This is the first and greatest commandment.

39 And the second is just like it:

Love your neighbor as yourself.

40 All the Torah and the preaching of the prophets
depends on these two commandments."

The miracles of Jesus

The second thing the apostles emphasized in trying to convince their fellow Jews that Jesus was the promised Messiah was the extraordinary events of his life which we today call miracles. The New Testament writers do not use the term "miracle" in the sense of an occult performance. They conceived them to be signs that God was with Jesus, that he was "approved" by God. They considered them as acts of God's love, not actions done simply because they were "miraculous." *Jesus was not God on display, but God on man's side.* "Men of Israel," St. Peter said to his listeners in his very first sermon, "Jesus of Nazareth was a man approved by God among you by the mighty deeds and signs God worked through him in your company, as you all know." (*Acts* 2:22) So important was this aspect in their preaching, that, when the gospels were composed (anywhere from 20 to 60 years after Jesus' death), the miraculous events occupy a major portion of the material—one-third of St. Mark's gospel deals in one way or another with the miracle events.

With their long history of looking upon the events of their lives as God's saving actions, the Jews looked upon the extraordinary events associated with a religious preacher's life as evidence of God's saving action in his *life*. It is not surprising, therefore, that the apostles preached about the things Jesus did, as a means of showing their listeners that he was the Messiah.

When the miracles of Jesus were recorded, the writers grouped several of these extraordinary events together, not to give the impression that they occurred at once,* but to preserve the memory of them and to impress their readers with the fact that Jesus was, indeed, "from God."

Perhaps some of the wonders Jesus performed were the healing effect of his strong personality on those who were psychologically ill, but the fact that we can "explain" some of these events in the terms of modern psychology does not do away with the fact that marvelous events did occur and they were taken as signs of God's love by those who were there. It is worth noting that the primitive Church rejected certain accounts of Jesus' life because the events there recorded were too fanciful, over-exaggerated, or highly imaginative presentations of the "miraculous." In the minds of the apostles, Jesus was not a sorcerer or magician putting on an empty display; to classify him as such was to distort his real nature and mission. He was a healer, a savior. His miracles had a benevolent style and purpose. They were as much "saving" as was his death. Curing was not a stunt to prove the power of his death but the "saving" itself being made apparent.

Whether the miracles mentioned by the apostles or recorded later in the gospels were curing the sick, increasing the amount of food, changing water into wine, relieving neurotic people of their anxieties, or calming the waves at sea, *they have but one purpose: to show Jesus as savior.* This fitted into their plans for convincing their hearers that Jesus of Nazareth was the promised Messiah. For them he was. The apostles understood that their mission in life was to convince other people that he was.

The death-resurrection event

The third major emphasis of the apostles and New Testament writers is on the death-resurrection event. Comparing the space given to this aspect of the life of Jesus with all other presentations, one would have to say that *this event is the most important*

---

* See, for example, *Mark* 1:21-45; 2:1-28; 3:1-12, where certain types of miracles are mentioned as if they had happened in sequence.

36

part of the New Testament proclamation of the kingdom of God.

The resurrection of Christ is paramount in Christian faith, not simply because Christ rose from the dead, but because of *what this means.*

For the disciples of Christ who experienced him alive after his death (as far as we know, nobody *saw* him rise from the dead), Jesus' resurrection gave new and complete meaning to his previous life. As astonishing as the thought of resurrection was merely as a physical fact, for the disciples it had a meaning far beyond that. Like the miracles of Christ, it was a sign of the *saving aspect* of Jesus' life and of the deeper meaning of his life in the saving plan of God. In the resurrection human salvation became evident.

The close followers of Jesus had certainly suspected that Jesus was unique. They had experienced his powerful personality, had been moved by his persuasion, had witnessed his miracles, had been awed by his total command of situations. They knew him to be a man beyond all other men, they knew that if anyone had had an answer to life's mystery, certainly the man Jesus had. They were grateful for their experience with him, but were saddened by his death—overwhelmed by the turn of events.

When, right after his death, they returned to their meeting place "to pick up the pieces," they were discouraged, afraid, uncertain. On the morning of the third day no one could have persuaded them that the future held anything for them, especially as far as Jesus was concerned. But the unexpected re-appearance of Jesus changed all that.

The record of the events concerning the resurrection is necessarily confused—as is the reporting of any event of world-shaking importance. Luke's account says the apostles first heard the news from the women who had gone to give the body of Jesus proper burial care. John's account says that Mary Magdalene visited the tomb first, saw the empty tomb and ran to tell Peter and John that someone had taken the body away. Mark's account tells that the women who went to the tomb "ran away . . . shaking and overcome with fear, and said nothing to anybody, for they were afraid." For the apostles and later for the writers, the exact details were not as important as the event they were recounting. As they told it, Jesus was indeed alive—he had come back from the dead—for they had talked with him, had eaten with him, not once, but several times. For them, the resurrection was a fact.

After the first shock of their experience of Christ's resurrection, the meaning of his resurrection gradually came to them. It recalled to their minds their earlier suspicions about his uniqueness. He had been great, he had been unique, he had been the most extraordinary person they had met. But now, in light of the resurrection, a whole new dimension had been added to their conception of him as a man. Suddenly everything he had said and done took on this new light. Suddenly, everything fitted! Suddenly they realized that their Jesus was the Promised One, the Messiah, the Christ, the Lord. Quick as a flash, they grasped the totality of their experience. Jesus was the Son of God.

When they realized this, they *had* to tell others. They had to share the good news. Their uncertainty, their fear, their hesitancy, their realization of their own limitations left them, and they went out to tell everybody that Jesus was the Lord.

The resurrection of Jesus completely changed their lives, and their positive conviction that Jesus was the Lord shaped the form and the content of their message. They were trying to get everyone *to believe* that Jesus was the Messiah—and they told it as it was, shaping the message to bring out the meaning. They interpreted everything in the light of the resurrection. What it meant was gradually made clear to them and to those after them who believed in Jesus.

The resurrection was a sign of hope. It made clear that both the present and the future were eminently worthwhile. It showed that there was a future—some kind of life beyond the grave—a place or state where all mankind would experience a new life, a life shared with God. It stripped away the hazy notions of life after death and gave certainty to the hope of immortality that lingered in all men's consciousness. And for Christians it established the hope of the resurrection of the body—the belief that human beings as persons will live for eternity a whole new life that has none of the sorrow or uncertainty, the fear and the dread of mortal life.

The resurrection is the Christian answer to the question about life that everyone asks: what does it all mean? It makes sense out of the fates of earthly life and gives to Christians an answer beyond what they consider to be the limitations of the Marxist hope for this life, the anonymity of the Hindu Nirvana, or the material fulfillment of Islam. It gives Christian belief a force for this life and the next. It impels us to seize life as it is and make it better *now*. Christians believe that Jesus' resurrection enabled him to pass beyond the limitations of time and space and to live his new life forever. They believe that he lives and acts in his Church.

Because we believe that Jesus lives and acts in his Church, we believe that *eternity* (the shared life with God) *is now* and that our efforts must be bent to bringing about those conditions in our world which will enable men to share the divine life now. Catholic Christians believe that *the life of eternity can be achieved in part in this world* by the effort of Christians to live the risen life with Christ and to invite others to share it with them.

For Christians, this risen life shared with Christ is not an abstraction—it is meant to be a concretely felt reality. It must be *experienced* by mankind in the life they lead now. Christians do not believe that Faith alone will relieve the miseries of life (that is fatalistic) but that it gives man a reason for making his present world a better place. *Christians are not resigned to the condition of sickness, evil and death; they look upon these as challenges to be overcome.* They believe that the ultimate sin is selfishness, indifference, rejection of others and a refusal to try to ease the burdens of human suffering by the intellectual and technological gifts God has given man to work with. Hence, the Christian imperative of the resurrection is to work for a better world—a world where peace is a reality, where food and shelter and clothing are sufficient for all mankind, a world where the compelling force of man's actions is love, the love of Christ, a reflection of the love of God for his creation. When this occurs, God's initial plan, "let us make man to our image and likeness,"* will be a reality.

With the resurrection of Jesus as the key to their understanding of Jesus, the apostles were faced with the monumental task of convincing others of this meaning of the life of Jesus. They *believed* that Jesus was the Messiah, they *trusted* that what he had said about God and life were true, and they *were faithful* to that belief and trust in their own lives. It was their faith in Jesus that made them what they were. They went out to tell others the good news of salvation.

As time went on, and the circumstances permitted, more and more items from their remembered experiences came to the apostles. Eventually these were recorded in the gospels and reflected on in the epistles (the first recorded Christian theology).

---

* *Genesis* 1:26

This Scriptural material forms the basis and the ground of Christian belief, practice and worship. It is for this reason that the New Testament is the norm of Christian discussion.

Because his death and resurrection are so central to Christian belief, the preaching of the apostles necessarily contained the events of Christ's life which led up to his death. His betrayal and arrest were presented in a dramatic form. Both the apostles and the later writers were faced with the problem of why Jesus, a man they knew to be so great, was put to death. Hence, the story tells of a crisis situation.

In one sense, in the gospels, we have a "good guys" *vs.* "bad guys" presentation with the dramatist ignoring, as to some extent dramatically irrelevant, what does not tend to make the "bad guys" look "bad." The confrontation is presented as immediate and compelling, the issues are spelled out in black-and-white terms, the principal characters are brought face to face, and the result is strikingly presented.* What is missing, of course, as in any drama (because of the demands of the art-form), is anything that would lessen the focus on the conflict by diffusing attention to details not likely to heighten the sense of opposites.

In this sense, the account of Jesus' passion in the New Testament runs the risk of any piece of dramatic writing: historical over-simplification. There is a danger that the readers will think that the real human beings named in the theological drama were in life as simply all-good and all-bad as presented. This danger of accepting drama for history is very real and is attested to by the existence of anti-Semitism in the Christian community. Many times in the past and even in the twentieth century many Jewish people have been disliked and even persecuted by Christians. As such, anti-Semitism is un-Christian. Those who claim to find the basis for their anti-Semitism in the New Testament confuse the teachings of Jesus with the anti-Jewish interpretations which later writers frequently gave to them.

Even the smallest amount of thought and a minimum of research will show that not all the Jews of Jesus' time were bad (any more than all were good). Christians should look with sympathy on the dilemma of the Hebrew religious leaders of Jesus' time. They were faced with what they considered to be a real

---

* If you have studied *Macbeth,* you know that Shakespeare did the same thing to heighten the dramatic impact of the Macbeth historical events.

danger to the Hebrew religion (and as it turned out, it *was* a danger to their view of Jewish faith) because here was a man who challenged the "traditions of the ancients" (the whole interpretation of the Law as it was commonly understood at Jesus' time), who spoke on his own authority, who cut through the maze of rules and laws and practices and insisted on his own interpretation of the prophetic message.

For Christians, the real meaning of Jesus' death is not the persons or external circumstances that make up the Passion story. The real meaning is in *why Jesus chose to die*. As he tells us in the Last Supper scene, his death is a *sacrifice for mankind*.

The early Christians knew that Jesus was not the only man ever crucified (as painful and humiliating as it was), and they were not obsessed with trying to prove the "guilt" of those who put him to death. They were concerned with what Jesus' death meant for mankind.

The New Testament theology of Jesus' death as a saving act extends the Hebrew concept of man's sinful state and God's transcendent holiness. Atonement, an element in sacrificial death apparent in much of ancient literature, is there made central. Atonement, as a form of saving, is a saving of man from himself, a saving from the results of sin: the acts of an angry or just God. The "sacrificial death" of Jesus makes *the saving of man from himself* the center of religion.

In the Jewish practice of Jesus' day, sacrifice was made to God through a priest who represented the people by the offering of a gift, making it sacred by withdrawing it from a nonsacred use and directing it to God. The most common act of sacrifice was the slaying of an animal (for example, a lamb) and the sprinkling of its blood as a sign of its total giving to God. Often the sacrificial act was completed by a sharing (in a meal) of the flesh of the animal as a form of communion with God through the gift and with fellow worshipers through a common meal.

After Jesus' resurrection, the apostles saw his death as *the perfect sacrifice* to God offered for sinful man. That is why the death of Jesus was viewed by early Christians as a *triumph* (even though crucifixion by itself was degrading and intended as a sign of shame and punishment). For this reason, too, Christians used "the sign of the cross" as a sign of pride and recognition.

Early Christian references to Jesus as the "lamb of God," "the suffering servant" and the like, come from the idea of the

41

sacrificial death of Jesus. The Passover meal that the apostles shared with Jesus highlighted in their minds the element of his death as sacrificial.

Like the Jewish people they recalled that this was not just any meal or any celebration. It was not reducible to comaraderie or an emotional direction toward God. It was a special meal, a special action and a particular kind of gathering. For the Jewish people the Passover meal recalled the salvation of their ancestors from slavery in Egypt. For the apostles it became a sharing of the Lord's Body and in His sacrificial death, which saved mankind from the slavery of sin.

Matthew

26:26 While they were eating,
    Jesus took some bread,
    blessed, broke it, and gave it to his disciples
    and said, "Take this and eat.
    This is My Body."
27 Then taking the cup, he gave thanks
    and gave it to them, saying,
    "Drink this, all of you.
28 For this is My Blood of the New Covenant,
    which will be shed for many in forgiveness of sins."

From the very first days after Pentecost, the apostles gathered the Christians together and, after teaching them about Jesus and hearing the profession of the faith of these Christians, they held a memorial of Jesus by doing as he had directed them: sharing in the Body and Blood of Christ.*

It is from this practice (recalling the death of the Lord and sharing his Body and Blood) that the liturgy of the Catholic Church comes. No matter what the form is, no matter what rites and ceremonies accompany the Eucharistic Action, its basis is still the same: recalling the sacrificial death of Christ and the sharing in the sacrificial meal, the receiving of Holy Communion, Christ's Body and Blood.

When we Christians receive the Body and Blood of the Lord, we do not think of ourselves as receiving a dead Lord, but

---

* See St. Paul's first letter to the Corinthians, chapter 11, verses 17 to 34, for a specific reference to the sacredness and sacrificial aspect of the memorial in the early days of the Church.

The Sacrament of the Last Supper — Salvator Dali

the *living* Jesus. We *celebrate* his death, for we believe that he not only rose from that death but also is alive in us and celebrates it with and in us. It is a death which has won a new form of life for human beings—a share in divine life.

The God-man

How can a person share what he does not have? How could Jesus the Messiah share the life of God with us if it were not his to give?

Reflecting on this deepest meaning of Jesus' role as Risen Messiah—to share God's life with us—the Church has come to a clear understanding that Jesus is more than a mere man. While this awareness was vaguely present even in the first encounter of the apostles with the forceful personality of Jesus, it was not clarified with exact words until many years after Jesus had died.

Right after Jesus' death and resurrection, the apostles proclaimed that he was indeed the Messiah and the "Son of God." At first they did not have a systematic theological explanation of how Jesus could be both human and divine. Systematic explanations came later, as theologians worked on the problem for centuries. But in the earliest beginnings of Christianity, the apostles proclaimed that Jesus was the person who best fitted the Hebrew expression "Son of God."

This led them to further thought about the meaning of Jesus and what role he had played in the salvation plan of God. Thus, instead of simply preaching what Jesus did, they began to *theologize* about Jesus, which naturally led them to conclude that, if he was the true *Messiah,* he was *the* Son of God, not just a person specially dedicated to God.

Only gradually, therefore, did they come to the point where it was clear to them how Jesus was more than Messiah in the traditional sense, more than other "sons of God." Only gradually could they come to declare that Jesus was truly the Word of God, the Word made flesh, the Word who was God—as the Gospel according to John proclaims:

1:1 In the beginning there was The Word.
The Word was in God's presence,
and The Word was God.

2 He was with God from the beginning.

3 Everything was made through Him,
and without Him, nothing created ever happened.

4 In Him was Life,
and this Life was mankind's light.

14 And The Word became flesh
and pitched His tent among us;
and we saw His glory,
glory belonging to The Father's Only Son,
full of love and faithfulness.

Our Christian belief as Catholics that Jesus is the Son of God, the Second Person of the Trinity, is a response of *faith*. The divinity of Christ cannot be proved scientifically or historically (as, for example, we can prove the existence of the man Jesus or his human impact). This, after all, is what faith is all about. If a thing can be verified, or circumstantial evidence points indisputably to a conclusion, faith is not present. It arises *from* an experience, it is true, but the truth of our faith is not conclusively proved by experience. It is a "knowing beyond knowing" as described in Chapter 2.

As Catholics, we Christians believe that Jesus is God acting humanly. We *know* the apostles experienced Jesus as a man; we *believe* that Jesus is God because we believe with the apostles that this man, Jesus, was more than a unique person, more than a prophet, more than simply one of the great religious leaders of history. This belief (and our acceptance of him as divine) is what makes Jesus incomparable to other great religious figures (Moses, Mohammed, Confucius, Buddha, and so on). It puts him, as a man, in a class by himself.

The conviction that Jesus is a divine person (or God expressing himself humanly) came gradually. The preparation for this conviction, of course, was the apostle's experience of Jesus as a man. It did not just pop up, formed (as some have contended) as a substitute psychosis for their disappointment over his death.

The acceptance by the apostles of Jesus as risen from the dead was very gradual, very halting.* Only after several divergent

---

* See, for example, the resurrection accounts in *Matthew* 28, *Mark* 16, *Luke* 24, *John* 20 and *Acts* 1.

encounters did the apostles accept the risen Jesus. And why not? Who could believe such a thing without solid experience of the risen Jesus? But once they had been convinced, their view of Jesus and their understanding of his mission changed. Suddenly they saw their own lives in a new light. Thereafter Jesus was *Lord*.

Because of this, they "read back" into their experiences, and into his words as they remembered them, meanings which they now understood although they once did not understand them. This does not mean, of course, that the historical Jesus was one person and the Christ of their faith was another, any more than your failure to recognize a friend at a masquerade party makes two different persons of your friend. The only thing that had changed was that the apostles had a deeper awareness of who Jesus really was; their experience now took on an aspect they had not suspected or thought about before.

After their Pentecost experience, the apostles (and later the writers of the New Testament) were able to understand the history of the Hebrews, the waiting for the Messiah, and the salvation plan of God in the light of the person of Jesus, who now became clearly in their eyes the Christ, the Anointed One, the Savior. This consciousness of the early Christian community of the role of Jesus in the Divine Plan of Salvation is best summed up in St. Paul's letter to the Ephesians:

Ephesians

1:3 Blessed be God the Father of Our Lord Jesus Christ
who has blessed us in Christ . . .
4 and chosen us in Him
even before the world was founded . . .
9 He has made known to us the secret of His will,
according to His good pleasure,
which He had all along,
10 to bring His plan to fulfillment
when the times were ripe,
to bring all things to a head in Christ,
both the things in heaven and those on earth.
22 He has placed everything at His feet
and made Him head of the whole church,
which is His body and His completion—
and He is the fulfillment of everything.

History as focused in Christ

Life as we experience it is forward-moving. Things happen to us and we respond; people come into our lives and we respond. We grow through our responses. We learn from the things that happen to us; we make friends and grow in friendship with the people in our lives. Each of us has a personal history of growing, changing, developing because of what happens and whom we meet.

Mankind at large also has a history. Things have been happening in the universe; great persons have been showing up in history. Mankind has learned from the happenings of the past; mankind has grown deeper by responding to the great persons. When primitive man accepted an unknown cave man's invention of the wheel, history was changed. When men learned to love the poetry of Homer or to enshrine the sculpture of Phidias or to preserve the writings of Aristotle, mankind as a whole benefited. We have all learned to appreciate beauty and truth to a greater degree because of our responses to these great men.

It is not surprising then that history should have been dramatically changed by the entrance of Jesus into the world. Even without Christian faith, we can see the enormous impact this religious prophet had on the world; the existence of the Christian church is a fact. But with the eyes of Christian faith, we can see the most fitting reason for Jesus' impact on world history. *If we believe Jesus is God in Person as a man among men, we believe that mankind's response to this Man is crucial for world history.*

47

Our response to any other great man's wisdom or art or achievement may make us wiser or more sensitive or more productive; but our response to The Word can make us "sons of God"—can make us all that man can hope to become.

Our Christian tradition tells us that God's personal appearance in human history was not an accident, not an afterthought on God's part. Christians believe God had been preparing history for his coming, and is still working in history through the Christ-community to bring to completion the final age of the world which Christ inaugurated.

Thus, we see the life, death, and resurrection of Jesus as the *focus* of history. We see it is the *one* event that makes sense out of everything else that has happened in history. We see everything else before Christ as leading to his coming, and everything after Christ as an extension of his coming. Seeing history this way is an act of faith. Only when we see history this way does our Christian community make sense to us. **We are the community which responds to God in history and therefore responds to God in Christ, the focus of history.**

From the point of view of our faith, the world's history can be divided into four phases:

1. Creation and primitive history.
2. Covenant-history before Christ.
3. The Christ event.
4. Covenant-history after Christ.

In these booklets on *The Emerging Church* we will concentrate on phase 4. But here let us briefly describe all four phases.

Creation and primitive history

Today we live in a scientific world where the discoveries of science are part of our mental outlook. In today's world of scientific culture, we are accustomed to think of the history of the world as something that extends far back into the past, long before the human race as we know it was in evidence. Most people in the developed nations of the world accept the story of evolution as a scientifically established fact. We are at home with our mental picture of the universe beginning in a primitive cosmic state eons ago and forming itself into stars and galaxies, one of which is our own solar system with the planet Earth forming and cooling maybe four billion years ago. We are familiar with the account of molecules combining in more and more complex forms until one day, perhaps two billion years ago, the first self-reproducing protein occurred in some now-forgotten ocean. We know the story of life's evolution to higher and higher forms of consciousness. Without knowing exactly what happened in between or where it happened, our scientific consciousness sees that, sometime before 1,000,000 B.C., the highest form of life known on earth was a set of fairly erect-walking apes called "hominids" (near-men); and it envisions, sometime after 1,000,000 B.C., communities of what we now recognize as men because they had made fire a tool, had painted animals in caves, and had sharpened rocks for weapons.

We know that, from a very early age, these communities of prehistoric men were aware of a Force or Forces greater than themselves and that they engaged in rituals to respond to this Force or Forces. When this human community appeared, a break-through* occurred in the universe.

Our faith does not find this scientific story of human origins meaningless, but *interprets* it from the point of view of God's activity. The response of our faith to science's account of prehistory is: *If* it happened this way, then it was the work of God.

Christians believe that when the time was ripe, God made men more and more conscious of His presence and His activity through His favorite instrument: man. Through man's own ex-perience and reflection, other men were awakened to wiser ex-perience and deeper reflection, which in turn provoked yet more modified experience and still greater reflection in other men, until

---

* Every major step in evolution is called a breakthrough, for it is entirely unpredictable. From the data on hand, no one could predict that each advance would come from the existing previous form. Scientifically viewed, these new forms had no observable potential within them to produce the next form. We can look back at the evolutionary process and say, "Of course," but strictly speaking, though that which a thing becomes is con-tained in that which it was, it is not a true breakthrough unless a phenome-non different in kind rather than degree appears. The entire evolutionary process portrays this phenomenon whether it is biological, economic, cultural or ecclesiastical.

religion had become a definite and elaborate part of primitive human life.

When the human community had been brought by God to bring itself to a point where it could accept another breakthrough, the second phase of faith-history began.

Covenant history before Christ

Because Christianity has its roots in Judaism, Christians accept the Jewish interpretation of history, citing its beginning as the call of Abraham and his clan to leave the system of many nature gods and cling to his own one God.

From these pre-Jewish roots, Hebrew religion survived and developed until the time of the Exodus event, when Moses and his people swore a Covenant in the desert to Yahweh as their National God.

Having arrived in Canaan, the people continued to deepen in understanding of God and His way of dealing with men through the preaching of the prophets, whom Christians as well as Jews remember as being specially inspired by God.

In the history of the Jewish people, Christians see God's action in the world coming into focus: they see God revealing Himself gradually, respecting the freedom of mankind to question, search, discard false ideas, and gradually come to less inadequate ideas of Him.

The Christ event

Christians believe that the high point of God's self-revelation is the God-man: Jesus. They believe that creation in and through man was from the beginning called to participate in the divine life and that it was saved in Christ from man's waywardness as epitomized and expressed in the *Genesis* story of the fall. In

Christ, God is seen both as making a personal appearance in creation and as assuring, despite and through man's freedom, that creation in man will love God in the way that He intended from the beginning. They believe that when the world was ready—through long ages of development—the Word became incarnate. And through this Incarnation, creation was given its true meaning, the sharing of divine life.

Christians see as the "redemptive act" of Christ not simply his coming, not only his death on the cross, but his *total life:* his life in his mother's womb, his birth, his childhood, adult life, sufferings, death, and especially his resurrection. The resurrection, after all, is the startling thing about the life of Christ. If Christ rose from the dead, it was the same Christ risen to a new life—a resurrected life. It is the risen Christ, the "new-life" Christ, that Christians believe lives and acts through his Spirit in his followers, the Church.

This is the uniqueness of the Christian faith. Christians believe not only that God became man, but that this Jesus is alive and acts in the Church. Christians do not believe in a dead hero, a mighty healer, a great preacher, to be admired and imitated much in the same fashion as any dead hero, but in a real person who, somehow, lives in his followers and shares his risen life with them. This is where Christians part company with believers in all other religious groups. Christians respect others' beliefs, share their concerns, feel their hurts and rejoice in their triumphs. But as Catholics, we Christians also believe that Christ is divine and that in Christ God shares his life with men.

Covenant history after Christ

The apostles and first followers of Jesus were convinced that with the coming of Jesus the Kingdom of God had been established and they had been sent to announce it. The Church remembers that they began their preaching immediately after the Pentecost happening. From this time through the present moment and beyond is called by Christians the "Christian era" because, although it is after the historical life of Jesus, *it is considered an*

51

*extension of his life into the community.** This phase of history is the time in which our Catholic Church exists.

The roughly 1900 years since Pentecost can be subdivided in many ways, but for the survey purposes of this booklet we have chosen to divide the history of the Catholic Church into six periods. Each represents an era in world history when the Church reached a new breakthrough in its understanding of itself and its mission in the world.

1. Jewish Christianity (Pentecost to about 100 A.D.)
   The small group of Jewish believers decides how the Christian life is related to Jewish life.

2. Christianity Established (100 A.D. to about 500 A. D.)
   The believers, now coming from all ranks of Greco-Roman society, decide how the Christian life is related to pagan rites and political religion.

3. Reconstruction Christianity (500 A.D. to about 1000 A.D.)
   After the barbarian invasions topple the Western Roman Empire, Christians create a new civilization among the descendants of the barbaric tribes.

4. Medieval Christianity (1000 A.D. to about 1500 A.D.)
   The Church in the West is the center of a highly civilized society's economy, politics, and culture.

5. Renaissance Christianity (1500 A.D. to about 1700 A.D.)
   The thrust toward personal and political freedom in the Western world divides the Christian Church into "Protestant" and "Roman Catholic" Christianity.

---

* Most Western calendars today divide history into B.C. (Before Christ) and A.D. (*Anno Domini,* Latin for "the year of the Lord"). This system of numbering the years dates from the Middle Ages, when the Western world was mostly Christian. Today's world, however, is pluralistic and many other calendars (such as the Jewish calendar and the Moslem calendar) do not divide history this way. Many Jewish people use the Western calendar but refer to the before-and-after-Christ periods as B.C.E. (Before the Common Era) and C.E. (Common Era). Perhaps the various cultural groups in the world will one day agree on a common calendar and numbering system; if they do, it will probably not be the Western calendar or any of the other religious calendars, but some kind of "scientific" calendar.

6. (a) Modern Christianity (1700 to about 1960 A.D.)
The rapid development of secular society's economics, politics, and culture creates a crisis in religious understanding and leads to a breakthrough called Vatican II.

(b) The Catholic Church in America (1500 A.D. to 1960 A.D.)
The thrust for personal and religious freedom achieved in the American political experiment and adopted by the American Catholics brings new understanding to the universal Church.

We do not discuss in this booklet the details of Church history in the period from 1960 on (a period which more and more writers are beginning to call "post-modern"). The Church in these times is in a new age of transition. The best sources of detail about this age are current magazines, news media, the documents of Vatican Council II, the decisions of present Church authorities, the experience of living Christians, and so on. The history of post-modern Christianity is still being made, and the older you grow the more you will have a part in making that history. Other booklets in this series will help you understand the post-modern world of trans-civilization and help you clarify the kinds of decisions yet to be made. But the Church cannot describe the unknown Christian future; it can only invite you to help create it.

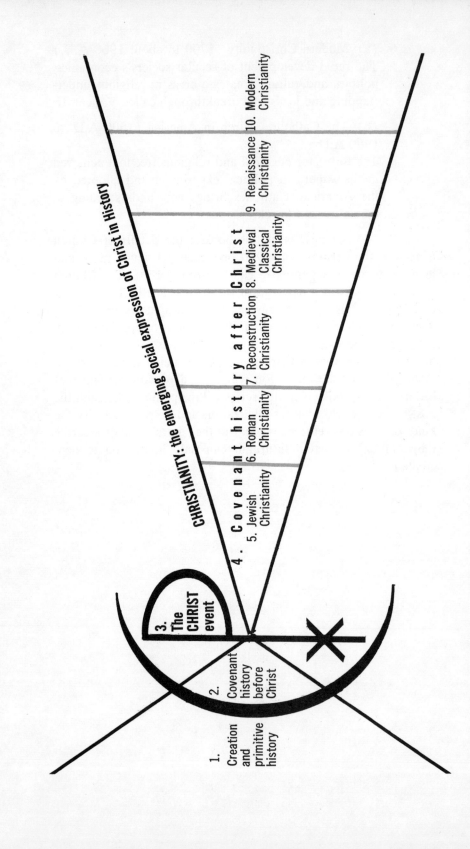

CHRISTIANITY: the emerging social expression of Christ in History

4. Covenant history after Christ

3. The CHRIST event

2. Covenant history before Christ

1. Creation and primitive history

5. Jewish Christianity

6. Roman Christianity

7. Reconstruction Christianity

8. Medieval Classical Christianity

9. Renaissance Christianity

10. Modern Christianity

CHRISTIANITY: THE EMERGING SOCIAL EXPRESSION OF CHRIST IN HISTORY

ORLANDO CABANBAN

Christianity and culture

As you discuss the history of the Christian Church as it is presented in the following pages, you will become aware of four important factors which have made the Church what it is today and which will help to shape it for the future: 1) There has been a gradual development in understanding the meaning of Jesus. 2) Christianity has affected whatever culture it moved into, and the culture has affected the expression and practice of the Christian faith. 3) No single culture best expresses the meaning of Jesus for all mankind. 4) Christianity at any given period in history is partly the product of that period of history.

These four principles are central to the history of the Church because they are part of any historical process and because the Church is a living community of believers who express themselves culturally. The history of any people is the history of the interaction of the economic, political and cultural forces which have shaped them; hence, the history of the Church is the history of the effect that Christianity has had on culture and culture upon Christianity.

Although we believe that Christianity is more than a cultural force of human making, we recognize that it must express itself culturally. This is at once its strength and its weakness. Because it is not dependent upon a particular culture, it can express itself in a variety of ways, each of which is authentic Christianity as long as it remains faithful to its mission. But, because it must express itself culturally, it will exhibit the limitations of its cultural expression. Hence, it will never reach its ideal state as long as the created world as we know it exists.

There will always be a condition of tension between the real and the ideal. When you understand this, you will understand the dynamic nature of Christianity and its constant need for change and updating. You will begin to understand why the bishops at Vatican Council II referred to the Church as a "pilgrim Church in exile from the Lord," and why the title of this book is *The Emerging Church*.

The first culture into which Christianity moved was Judaism. Christianity has its roots in Judaism because Jesus was a Jew, a product of the Judaism of his time, and the Church's first leaders and members were Jewish. Both he and they thought, talked and acted as the devout Jews of their day thought, talked, and acted.

When the first Jewish Christians moved outside of the spheres of Jewish culture and were confronted with Syrian, Egyptian, Greek, Roman and African cultures, they found that they had to express their understanding of Jesus in terms that were intelligible to people with non-Jewish language forms, philosophies, outlook and habits. As the Christian sphere of influence broadened, it moderated and improved the culture of the people it influenced; it, in turn, was affected by the culture into which it came. The same exchange of influences occurred in succeeding ages of history.

This interaction of Christianity and culture explains why the Church expresses itself as it does today, and why it will express itself in the future in terms of the society in which it will survive. As various cultures blend and are modified by contact with each other, and as the world moves more and more toward a planet culture and away from purely regional cultures, the Church will continue to be the social expression of Christ in history but in the terms of the planet culture that will emerge.

Jewish Christianity

Although we now experience Christianity as a world-wide religion, the apostles and first followers of Jesus were not concerned about the global impact of Christianity! Their first preoccupation was how to convince those of Jesus' countrymen who had seen him that he really was the Jewish Messiah. The first Christians were a distinct minority within the Jewish population and were only one of at least twenty-four groups in the country at that time proclaiming that a Messiah was about to deliver them from the evil of Roman domination.

Why the apostles were successful and others were not is a puzzle to historians who do not have our faith orientation. Christians believe that the reason lies in the plan of God for man's salvation. Christians believe that God operates in the world through His Spirit, and they believe that the Spirit acts directly in and through the Christian community. They believe that He acts through the normal channels of creation; that is, chiefly through the conscious activity of chosen human beings. Christians express their belief this way: God expressed Himself *creatively* in the universe He made; He expressed Himself *humanly* in the person of Jesus; He expresses Himself *dynamically* in the activity of the Spirit in the world.

This conviction about the Spirit of God acting in the Christian community comes to us from the very first experience of the apostles, who were convinced that their success came, not from what they did by themselves, but from what the Spirit of Jesus did through them. That is why, in the *Acts of the Apostles,* written by St. Luke sometime after 70 A.D., in the account of the first days of the apostle's preaching, the stress is on the Spirit of God. This account is an interesting example of biblical theologizing about an event in the life of the People of God interpreted to give evidence of God's action.* What the exact details of those first days were, we do not know. What we do have is an account of the growth in the number of believers and the divine reason for that growth.

St. Peter and the original apostolic preaching

Acts of the Apostles

2:1 When Pentecost time came around,
    they were all together in the same place.
  2 Suddenly there was a noise in the sky
    like a violent breath of wind,
    and it filled the whole house where they were staying.
  3 And separating tongues of fire settled upon each of them.
  4 They were all filled with the Holy Spirit
    and began to talk in various languages
    which the Holy Spirit gave them power to speak.

Whatever happened on that day, those present suddenly became aware of the real meaning of Christ, and they attributed this new understanding to the Holy Spirit.

The effect of this new awareness on the followers of Jesus was to move them from discussion of their problems (*Acts* 1) to an action-oriented apostolate. They went out to the people to tell them of their convictions about Jesus. The *Acts of the Apostles* is our Scriptural record of what happened:

Acts

2:5 Now in Jerusalem there were living
    devout Jews from every nation under heaven.
  6 With this outcry going on, a crowd gathered
    and were puzzled that each heard them

---

* We find a similar example of emphasis in the creative accounts of *Genesis*. The writer of *Genesis* continually stresses God's action to impress upon the Jewish people of his time that the Jewish God was not like the pagan gods, that He was a good God who did good things for mankind and that He and He alone was the creator of the world.

speaking his own language.

7 They were all amazed and said in wonder,
"Aren't all these speakers Galileans?
8 Then how come each of us has heard
the language we were born in?
12 . . . What do you suppose this all means?"
13 But some scoffers said,
"It means they've been drinking too much."
14 Peter, however, stood his ground with the Eleven
and shouted out: . . .
15 "These men aren't drunk, as you think—
it's only nine o'clock in the morning!
16 No, this is what the prophet Joel was talking about:
17 'At the end of the world, God says,
I will pour out a share of My Spirit on all men . . .
18 and they will speak in My name!'
22 You men of Israel, listen to me:
Jesus of Nazareth—
a man whom God certified before your eyes
with miracles, wonders, and signs . . .
23 this man was handed over
in God's deliberate plan and foreknowledge
to be crucified and killed. . . .
24 But God has raised him up,
loosening death's grip—
in fact, it was impossible for death to hold onto him!
36 Now, let all Israel know it without a doubt:
God has made this man Jesus the Messiah and Lord!"
37 Hearing this, they were deeply moved
and asked Peter and the other apostles,
"Brothers, what must we do?"
38 Peter then told them,
"Change your outlook on life completely—
and be baptized, everyone of you,
in Jesus Christ's name for the forgiveness of your sins.
Then you will receive the Holy Breath of Life!"
41 Those who took his word were baptized,
and there were added that day about three thousand souls.*

---

* In ancient writing numbers are used to indicate the importance of an event. The author of *Acts* is here indicating how important this event was in the minds of the first Christians.

With the Pentecost event as their starting point, the apostles began their preaching first in Jerusalem, then in the provinces. It was hard work. Some believed them; others did not. Naturally there was skepticism (how would you feel if someone came along and said that so-and-so was the Christ?), and in certain official areas there was outright opposition. This came to a head when Peter and John healed a cripple on the stairs of the Temple.

Acts

4:1 While they were still talking to the people,
some priests and Sadducees and the Temple officers
came up,

2 disturbed that they were teaching the people
and announcing the resurrection of the dead in Jesus.

3 They laid hands on them and threw them in jail
until the next day, for it was now evening.

4 But many who had heard The Word believed;
and the number grew to five thousand.

5 The next day their rulers and elders and scribes
were convoked in Jerusalem

6 along with Annas the high priest
and Caiphas, John, and Alexander
and whoever was from the priestly class.

7 Standing them in their midst, they interrogated them:
"By what right or in whose name have you done this?"

8 Filled with the Holy Spirit, Peter answered them:
"Leaders of the people, and senior citizens, listen:

9 If we are on trial today about the healing of a cripple:
in whose name was he saved?

10 Then let it be known to all of you and all of Israel:
it was in the name of the Lord Jesus
the Messiah from Nazareth
. . . that this man stands before you healed.

12 There is no salvation in anyone else;
nor is there any other name under heaven given to men
in which we must be saved."

13 Seeing the confidence of Peter and John,
and remembering they were not very well educated,
they were amazed and they recognized them
as having been with Jesus.

14 But seeing the man who had been cured

standing right there with them,
they were powerless to contradict them.

¹⁵ So they ordered them to wait outside the council room
and debated among themselves:

¹⁶ "What are we going to do with these men?
A great sign has certainly happened through them,
the whole population of Jerusalem knows about it,
and we can't deny it.

¹⁷ But we must command them
not to broadcast it any further among the people
and not to preach to anybody any more in this name."

¹⁸ Calling them back in,
they ordered them to stop preaching and teaching
in Jesus' name.

¹⁹ But Peter and John answered them back,
"You be the judges whether it is right in God's eyes
for us to listen to you rather than to God.

²⁰ We simply can't be quiet
about the things we have seen and heard."

²¹ So they dismissed them,
since because of the crowd
they could not find a way to punish them;
for everyone was glorifying what had taken place.

²² The man in whom this wonder had been done
was over forty years old.

In spite of the warnings, the apostles kept right on talking about Jesus.

Once again they were arrested, and when the trial was about to begin . . .

Acts

^{5:22} The guards came and opened the cell
but couldn't find them.
They went back and reported,

²³ "We found the cell completely locked
and guards in front of the doors,
but when we opened it up there was nobody inside."

²⁴ Listening to these statements,
the Temple officer and ruling priests
tried to figure out what had happened.

²⁵ Just then a messenger came to tell them,

"Those men—the ones you put in jail—
they're standing in the Temple teaching the people."

26 So the officer went with his policemen
and abducted them, but without force
(lest they be stoned by the people).

27 And they brought them back to the council room.
The high priest interrogated them:

28 "Didn't I give you strict orders
not to teach in this name?
And here you have filled Jerusalem with your teaching
and you want to bring this man's blood down on our heads!"

29 Peter and the apostles replied,
"We have to obey God rather than men.

30 The God of our ancestors has raised Jesus up . . . !

31 God has raised him to his own right hand
for the conversion of Israel and the forgiveness of sins.

32 And we are the witnesses to these words—
we and the Holy Breath of Life,
whom God has given to those who obey Him!"

33 When they heard this they were enraged
and had thoughts of murdering them.

34 But one of the council members rose up:
a Pharisee named Gamaliel,
a popularly revered doctor of the Torah.
He ordered the men to be taken outside a little while
and then he addressed the assembly:
"Men of Israel, wait and see about these men.
Remember Theodas who said he was somebody,

36 and the four hundred men who followed him—
all those who believed in him were routed
and reduced to nothing.

37 And after him, Judas of Galilee
stood out for a while in publicity
and got the people to follow him—
he too perished and all his followers disbanded.

38 So I tell you now,
stay away from these men and let them go their way;
for if this business is a merely human affair,
it will fall apart.

39 But if it is really from God,
you won't be able to break it up

64

—unless you want to find yourselves fighting God."
They agreed with him.

40 Then they had the apostles brought back in,
whipped them, and ordered them
not to speak in the name of Jesus,
and dismissed them.

41 But the apostles went away from the council glad
that they had been found worthy to şuffer
in the name of Jesus.

42 And every day, in the Temple and in private homes,
they never stopped teaching and preaching
the Good News of Jesus the Messiah.

How did the apostles and their friends live? What did these men, most of whom were from the quiet northern province of Galilee, do to stay alive? According to the only record we have (the *Acts of the Apostles*), they went every day to the Temple to speak to the people who were there, to offer sacrifice and to pray. They went to private homes where people gathered to hear them tell about Jesus. They slept in a common house, they ate with their friends, they visited among the converts, and "assembled for the breaking of the bread" (The Lord's Supper) at regular intervals.

They lived a normal Jewish life. Their habits, customs, language and religious practices were devoutly Jewish. They said Jewish prayers, sang traditional Jewish songs, celebrated the Jewish holidays, and observed the Jewish sabbath and rituals which so controlled the daily life of every devout Jew. There was nothing to distinguish them from the ordinary Hebrew in Jerusalem except that they were constantly talking about the man Jesus.

Gradually they began to have some effect upon the Jews of Jerusalem. (Some of the apostles, of course, had by this time moved to other major Jewish communities, but we don't have a record of them.) Within a relatively short time—perhaps two or three years—there were probably a few hundred Jews in Jerusalem alone who believed in Jesus, and enough in other cities to convince the Jewish leaders that something should be done about it. Among those given the responsibility of preventing the Jewish Christians from teaching about Jesus was a young, zealous, bright Jew named Saul. It was this Saul who was to become the apostle Paul, even though he was not one of the "original twelve" and had most likely never even seen Jesus.

St. Paul and the development of doctrine

Paul was a Jew who was a Roman citizen born in Tarsus in Cilicia, a Roman province on the eastern shore of the Mediterranean, some 400 miles north of Jerusalem. He had been educated in Jerusalem in the religious doctrine of the Pharisaic school of Judaism. He was one of its most ardent and fiery advocates, and he took it on himself—as his personal commitment—to stamp out the heretical sect, the Christ-followers. He admitted as much in his letter to the Christians at Galatia (54 A.D.):

Galatians

1:11 I want you to know, my brothers,
    that the Good News I preach
    is not a human invention—
12 for I did not receive it or learn it from any man,
    but by a revelation of Jesus Christ.
13 Surely you have heard about my way of life as a Jew,
    how I used to persecute the Church of God violently
    and tried to drive it out of existence.
14 I was more zealous for Judaism than many others my age,
    fanatically attached to the traditional ways of our ancestors.
15 But then it pleased Him, who by His favor
    had planned a special calling for me
    even while I was in my mother's womb,
    to reveal His Son in me,
16 that I might preach His Good News to the gentiles.
    And at once, not consulting flesh and blood,
17 I didn't even go to Jerusalem
    where my predecessors the apostles were;
    but I went away into Arabia
    and later returned to Damascus.
18 Finally after three years
    I came to Jerusalem to see Peter,
    and I stayed with him fifteen days.
19 I haven't seen any other apostle
    except the Lord's cousin James.
20 I swear to God that what I am writing to you is not a lie.
21 After that I went to parts of Syria and Cilicia.
22 There the Jewish churches in Christ

El Greco: "Saint Paul"

did not recognize me by face;

²³ they had only heard about me:
"The one who used to persecute us
is now preaching as Good News
the faith he once tried to exterminate."

²⁴ And they glorified God in me.

How this happened to St. Paul, the *Acts of the Apostles* tells us:

Acts

⁹·¹ Breathing murderous threats
against the Lord's disciples
Saul went to the high priest

² to ask for letters to the synagogue at Damascus—
that if he found any men and women of this sect,
he could bring them in chains to Jerusalem.

³ Now while he was on his journey
and drawing near Damascus,
suddenly a brilliant light from the sky surrounded him.

⁴ He fell to the ground and heard a Voice:
"Saul, Saul, why are you persecuting Me?"

⁵ "Who are You, Lord?" he asked.
It answered, "I am Jesus whom you are persecuting."
Trembling and astonished, he asked,
"Lord, what do You want me to do?"

⁶ The Lord told him, "Get up and go on to the city;
there you will be told what to do."

⁷ Now the men who were along with him
were standing there astonished;
they heard the Voice but saw no one.

⁸ Then Saul got up from the ground;
but when he opened his eyes he couldn't see.
And they led him by the hand into Damascus.

⁹ He was there three days unable to see,
and he didn't eat or drink.

¹⁰ Now at Damascus there was a disciple named Ananias,
whom the Lord called in a vision: "Ananias."
"I am here, Lord," he replied.

¹¹ The Lord told him, "Go on out to Straight Street
and look in Jude's house
for a man from Tarsus, named Saul.

¹³ But Ananias answered,

68

"Lord, I've heard a lot about this man:
the terrible things he's done
to Your friends in Jerusalem!
14 And he has authority from the ruling priests
to cart away anybody who invokes Your name!"
15 But The Lord told him,
"Go; he is My chosen messenger.
He will carry My name before peoples and kings
and the sons of Israel.
16 And I will show him many things to suffer for My name."
17 So Ananias went his way and entered the house;
laying his hands upon him, he said,
"Saul—brother—The Lord Jesus sent me,
The One who appeared to you on your journey.
You are to receive your sight
and be filled with the Holy Breath of Life."
18 At once a kind of scales fell from his eyes;
he received his sight;
and, rising up, he was baptized.
19 Then he accepted some food and regained his strength.
He stayed with the disciples in Damascus a few days,
20 immediately preaching in the synagogue
that Jesus is the Son of God.

It was after this that Paul's career as an apostle began. For nearly 35 years he traveled throughout the Roman Empire, setting up Christian communities in Rome and nearly every major city in Asia Minor and Greece. He first tried to convince his fellow Jews that Jesus was the Messiah, but later he went to the non-Jewish centers preaching about Jesus to whoever would listen to him. He was the most successful apostle.*

It is not only because Paul established so many Christian centers that the Church is indebted to him, however. *It is also because Paul is the first major Christian theologian*. It is from him that Christianity received its "Christology"** and its understanding of the meaning of Christ in the world.†

---

* See *2 Corinthians* 11:19-32.
** Theology which deals directly with Jesus Christ as Person. It might be called the science of the study of Jesus.
† It might be said that the original apostles preached the *Person* of Jesus in biographical form; but Paul preached the *meaning* of Christ in abstract form.

The importance of St. Paul's role in giving Christianity a formulation cannot be overestimated. It was from his understanding of the meaning of Jesus that the primitive Church was able to understand that it was more than a Jewish sect. It was the new People of God destined by divine intervention in history to bring mankind to salvation. After Jesus, St. Paul is the outstanding person in Christian history and the most influential.

What was Paul's basic thinking about Christ? It is probably best summed up in his famous letter to the Church at Ephesus.

Ephesians

1:3 Blessed be the God and Father of our Lord Jesus Christ,
who has blessed us
with every heavenly spiritual blessing in Christ,

4 since He chose us in Him
before the world was founded,
that we might be holy and clean in His eyes.

5 Because of love,
He planned beforehand of His own free will
to adopt us as sons through Jesus Christ and in Him,

6 all for the praise of His glorious favor
which was graciously bestowed on us in His beloved Son.

7 We are redeemed in Him by His blood,
we have our sins forgiven through His rich favor. . . .

9 He has made known to us the secret of His will,
according to His good pleasure,
which He had all along,

10 to bring His plan to fulfillment
when the times were ripe,
to bring all things to a head in Christ,
both the things in heaven and those on earth. . . .

13 Now you, too, have heard the Word of truth,
the Good News of your salvation in Him.
Believing in Him, you are marked
for the promise of the Spirit,

14 the pledge of what we shall inherit
when we gain our redemption
for the praise of His glory.

2:10 God has made us what we are:
created in Jesus Christ for the good way of life
which God has prepared as our path.

70

Before St. Paul the first preaching about Jesus, as we saw on pp. 59-65, concentrated on Jesus as Jewish Messiah. But St. Paul could hardly preach a Jewish Messiah to non-Jews—especially to Roman citizens, many of whom lived in the cities of Asia Minor and Greece where St. Paul preached. What was "Messiah" to them? What was Jesus saving *them* from? What was the role of Jesus in the non-Jewish world? Gradually it came to St. Paul: **Jesus was not simply a Jewish Messiah, he was the savior of the entire world.** St. Paul saw all of creation saved in Christ. He saw Jesus as the focus of history.

This theology of St. Paul was not developed overnight. It came from serious thought, growing out of the conviction of Jesus as savior and his own understanding of the meaning of Jesus as it developed in response to challenges to his message as he traveled from place to place and met people from all levels of society in many different cultures. St. Paul realized that Jewish thought forms and Jewish expressions were not the only way to present the meaning of Jesus. From his daring presentation the Church developed in its own understanding of the meaning of Jesus and of its mission.

The acceptance of the idea of Jesus as savior of all creation created a problem for the Church as it moved into non-Jewish cultures. This was the problem of the relationship of non-Jewish converts to Christianity and to the Jewish way of life.

Did Christians have to be Jews too?

As soon as St. Paul began to convert non-Jews in any great number, the inevitable question arose: did they have to observe the Jewish Torah? This question forced the leaders of the Church (the apostles) to answer a basic question which really hadn't come up when all converts to Jesus were Jews: What was the relationship of Christianity to Judaism? Their answer brought about an even clearer understanding of the world-wide meaning of Jesus.

The answer to both of these questions came relatively early in the life of the Christian community. The first question became

a prime issue within a few years and was settled for all time within the first twenty years of the Christian community, at the Council of Jerusalem in 49 A.D.*

Below is the scriptural record which summarizes the state of the question, the debates, and the conclusion of the Council. It is taken from the *Acts of the Apostles*.

Acts

15:1 Then some Christians came down from Judea
and taught the brothers,
"If you aren't circumcized according to the Torah of Moses,
you can't be saved."
2 Paul and Barnabus contradicted them
and a heated division of opinion arose.
So it was decided that Paul and Barnabas
and some representatives of the other side
should go up to the apostles and priests
in Jerusalem to settle this question.
3 Being sent on their way by the church,
they passed through Phoenicia and Samaria,
telling all about the conversion of the pagans,
to the great joy of all the brotherhood.
4 When they got to Jerusalem they were well received
by the church assembly, apostles, and elders,
and told them all about God's mighty deeds among them.
5 But some of the believers who were also Pharisees,
maintained, "They must be circumcized,
and taught to obey the Torah of Moses."
6 So the apostles and seniors met together
to look into this whole question.
7 After a great deal of debate,
Peter rose up to address them:
"Brothers, you know that from the earliest days

---

* This "first Council" established the general pattern for most subsequent Councils including Vatican II. In every Council the following features appear: 1) a general problem, 2) a meeting of the leaders (bishops), 3) open discussion of all sides of the problem, 4) a decision by the chief bishop, 5) an announcement of the conclusions. It is from this first meeting of the apostles to decide a major issue that we get our concept of "collegiality" (the sharing of authority among the leaders) and of papal "primacy" (the necessity of having a "president" of the assembly who speaks in the name of the group).

God in our midst chose some pagans
to hear the Good News from my own mouth and to believe.

8 And God, who reads the heart,
stood up for them as for us
through His Spirit.

9 He did not discriminate between them and us,
since they were purified in their hearts by faith.

10 Now then, why are you testing God,
trying to impose on the necks of the disciples
a burden that was too hard even for ourselves
and our ancestors to bear?

11 But we are saved the same way they are:
by the favor of the Lord Jesus Christ."

12 This quieted the council,
and they listened to Paul and Barnabas describe
the great signs and wonders God had worked through them
among the gentiles.

13 After they finished, James followed up:
"Brothers, listen to me.

14 Simon told you how from the first
God was present to draw from the pagans
a people in His own name.

15 The words of the prophets go along with this
where it is written,

16 '. . . I will rebuild the fallen House of David

17 . . . and all the rest of mankind shall seek the Lord,
all the pagans upon whom My name is invoked. . . ."

19 So I urge that we don't disturb
those who have turned to The Lord from pagan nations.

20 No, let's write to them
asking them not to eat meat
that has been offered to idols,
to stay away from sexual license,*
not to eat meat that has been strangled, or blood—

21 since on every sabbath this is commonly read
and preached in the synagogues
as Moses ordained from the most ancient times."

22 Then it met the approval
of the apostles and senior members
and the whole gathering,
to pick some men from their own ranks

(Judah, also called Barsabas, and Silas,
both leading members of the brotherhood)

23 and send them to Antioch with this written message:
"From the apostles and seniors in brotherhood
to the brothers in Antioch, Syria, and Cilicia: Greetings.
We have heard that some from among us
have been stirring up disquiet in your minds;
but they did not have authority from us.

25 So we, gathered together, have decided
to send these men to you:
our dear friends Barnabas and Paul,

26 men who have dedicated their lives
in the name of our Lord Jesus Christ.

27 And we are sending Judah and Silas to verify their words.

28 The Holy Spirit and we see fit
to impose no obligation beyond those necessary ones:

29 Don't eat meat
that has been offered to idols, or blood,
or meat that has been strangled,
and stay away from sexual license.*
It is sufficient to refrain from these things. Farewell."

30 So the group went, as they were sent, to Antioch
where they delivered the message
to the assembled congregation.

31 The community there was delighted with what they read.

The Council did not settle all the problems facing the
Christian community, of course, nor was everyone happy with
the decision. However, the first hurdle in self-understanding was
cleared, due to the insight and the persuasiveness of St. Paul and
his companion, St. Barnabas.

What was now clear, of course, was that followers of
Christ were not necessarily Jews and therefore they were not
bound by the Jewish Torah.**

---

* The word here translated "sexual license" probably refers to marriage between relatives, about which the Jewish rabbis were very strict. The other
three things are not wrong in themselves but the Christians who were for-
merly pagans are asked to refrain from these also out of consideration for
the sensibilities of the Jewish Christians.
** This is the entire way of life of the Jewish people including the regulations
governing the most minute details of daily living, the customs and practices
"handed down from the ancestors," and the interpretations by the scholars
and teachers.

This does not mean to say that Christians no longer observed any laws or that they made up laws to suit themselves individually. It means that mere observance of law as set down in the Torah, for them, was not the guarantee of salvation. Their faith was in the Person of Christ, not in the observance of the laws of the Torah as good as they might be.

The distinguishing features of Christianity

What distinguished the Christians from the Jews was their faith in Jesus, symbolized by the act of baptism, and their gathering for the "Lord's Supper." What distinguished them from their pagan neighbors was their attitude, outlook, motivation and practice of morality, as well as their faith in Jesus and their celebration of the Eucharist.

The "Lord's Supper," of course, is a reference to the Eucharist, to the Mass, as Catholic Christians now call it. *It is the most ancient and most distinguishable feature of the Catholic liturgy.* The first Christians came together to celebrate Christ among them, as he had asked them to do, by doing as he had done. Their celebration of the Eucharist was their way of participating in the sacrificial death of Jesus.

The earliest record we have of this Christian celebration is in St. Paul's first letter to the Corinthian Christians, which he wrote, interestingly enough, to correct some abuses which had cropped up:

1 Corinthians
> *11:20* Lately when you are gathering together
> it isn't for eating the Lord's Supper any more.
> *21* Everyone starts eating beforehand,
> and somebody is still hungry
> while somebody else is getting drunk.
> *22* Don't you have your own homes for eating and drinking?
> Are you trying to show contempt for the gathering
> by embarrassing those who are poor?
> What can I say to you?

76

You expect me to praise you? Not for this!

23 What I received from the Lord
is what I passed on to you:
how the Lord Jesus on the night of His betrayal
took some bread,

24 gave thanks for it, broke it, and said,
"Take this and eat.
This is My body to be handed over for you.
Do this in My memory."

25 And likewise, after He ate
He took the cup and said,
"This cup is the New Covenant in My blood.
Do this, whenever you drink it, in My memory."

26 Whenever you eat this bread and drink this cup,
you are showing forth the death of the Lord
until He comes.

This "coming together in the Lord," as St. Paul points out (we call it "going to Mass"), is to recall the sacrificial death of Christ and to clebrate the resurrection. It came, as you know, from the so-called Last Supper in which Jesus, in the setting of the Jewish Paschal Meal (the yearly celebration of the Jewish deliverance from Egypt), took the unleavened bread which was customarily distributed and, in addition to the usual prayers of thanksgiving, said, "This is my Body which will be given for you. Do this as a memorial of me."* At the end of the meal, using the traditional cup of wine offered in thanksgiving, Jesus passed it among his apostles and said, "Drink all of you from this; for this is my Blood, the Blood of the Covenant, which is poured out for many for the forgiveness of sins."**

It is interesting to note that the Christian moral way of life was not too distinguishable from the Jewish, except perhaps in its motivation. The Torah commanded that Jews love God and their neighbor. The many details concerning the smallest aspects of Jewish life had as their base respect for all created things. The Jewish Law was deeply concerned about justice (The "eye for an eye" concept was not intended as a cruel thing, but as a warning to God's people that no punishment should be harsher than the offense.) and about the reason for the Jewish

---

* *Luke* 22:19
** *Matthew* 26:27-28

Law: God commanded the Jewish way of life to keep the Jewish people from falling into the habits of their pagan neighbors. It prohibited especially idolatry, magical practices, disrespect for one's parents, and taking advantage of one's neighbor because of power, wealth or ambition. The problem was that as the Law was interpreted in Jesus' time, it had lost its real purpose, as usually happens when law becomes so picky, and was observed simply because it was the Law. The prevailing interpretation was that the Law by itself saved the Jews.

Jesus, in repeating the "two commandments" de-emphasized the law-for-the-sake-of-law idea, and restressed the original Jewish notion of the personal worth of each individual.* Jesus knew the intent of the law. He was well aware of the fact that Jewish law, in contrast to the laws of many neighboring nations, was intended to preserve the Jewish way of life and to protect the dignity and worth of each individual. In recalling this basic aspect of the law, Jesus was attempting to correct what he considered an abuse in the current interpretation of the law. Apparently he felt that the framework of the law and its present application prevented a devout Jew from showing real concern for his neighbor.

In this way Jesus taught his followers that, wherever the framework of the law really interfered with this concern, the law had to give way. The conflict between Jesus' idea and the mainstream of Jewish thought apparently rested on the difference between the need for meeting the existential situation (Jesus' way) and the need for observing the law until it was changed (the Jewish leaders' concept).

The problem, a constant challenge for all persons concerned with lawful society, boils down to the question of whether or not an individual can ever dispense with the law. Jesus felt that a person could under one condition: that the intent was based upon solid religious concern for the good of another. Jesus did not in any sense do away with the need for law. He knew that society depends on law, but he knew also that law applied without concern for the dignity of each individual could be oppressive. Ultimately, Jesus' vision of life showed him that man's freedom of conscience sometimes demands that he dispense with the law for the moment so that community good will be achieved.

Jesus' own personal self-integration (his own inner free-

---

* See, for example, *Luke* 10:25-37.

78

dom) enabled him to preach an ethical ideal that impelled his
followers to greater goodness. They could no longer simply keep
the external law of social necessity; they had to respond to the
inner necessity to be a real person. Jesus did not give laws to
be observed as ends in themselves or as measures of how "good"
each one was; he gave them as guidelines toward the ideals to
be striven for.

St. Paul expressed this mind of Christ as follows:

Romans

13:8 Don't accept any obligations to anybody
except to love one another;
for whoever loves his neighbor is fulfilling the law.
9 "Do not commit adultery,
do not kill or steal,
do not lie against anyone, do not be jealous"—
and any other commandment there might be—
it is all summed up in one statement:
"Love your neighbor as yourself."
10 If you love your neighbor
you will never do him any harm.
So the full completion of the law is love.

Leading the non-Jewish Christian converts from paganism to the Christian ideal of deep concern for their neighbors
was something else again. These converts did not have the ethical background of the Jewish converts, so St. Paul and the other
Christian leaders got down to brass tacks about certain things.
They reminded their Gentile converts that Jesus' ethical teaching was not some vague "love-in," but dealt with the nitty-gritty
of everyday relationships with people. They reminded them that
there were certain things which Christians did not do. For example, in his first letter to the Christians of Corinth,* St. Paul
wrote:

1 Corinthians

6:9 Don't you know that wrongdoers will not inherit
the kingdom of God?
Make no mistake about it—
nobody who fornicates or worships idols,

---

* A city in Greece so notorious for its depravity that the term "corinthian"
was a synonym for evil.

no adulterer or homosexual,
10 no thief or jealous person,
no drunkard or malicious-tongued person,
no extortioner is going to gain the kingdom of God.
11 You may indeed have been all these things;
but you have been washed clean,
you have been made sacred and right
in the name of our Lord Jesus Christ
and in our God's Breath of Life.
12 Even if everything were lawful for me,
that does not mean everything would be appropriate.
I will not let myself become the slave of anything,
even if it is all legal.
13 Let food be for the stomach and the stomach for food,
but God will eventually do away with both.
And the body is not for fornication,
but for The Lord, and The Lord for our body:
14 after all, God has raised up The Lord
and will raise us up too by His power.
15 You know, don't you,
that your bodies are members of Christ?
So shall I take the members of Christ
and make them members of a prostitute? Certainly not!
16 Don't you know that whoever embraces a prostitute
becomes one flesh with her?
—as it is written, "They will be two in one flesh."
17 But whoever embraces The Lord becomes one spirit.
18 Avoid fornication.
Most sins a man commits are outside his own body;
but a fornicator sins in his own body.
19 And of course you realize that your members
are the Temple of the Holy Breath of Life,
who is in you as your gift from God,
so that you really don't own yourself.
20 No, a great ransom has been paid for you;
so give praise to God and carry Him in your body.

In his letter to the Christians of Galatia—a Roman province in Asia Minor—St. Paul clarifies for his converts the difference between Christian liberty and moral irresponsibility. He stresses that *actions* are the test of a person's concern for the

80

real welfare of one's neighbor—actions that are motivated by the Spirit of Christ.

Galatians

4:13 You have been called to be brothers in freedom;
but don't hand this freedom over to slavery to the flesh;
instead, be servants of one another in love.

14 In fact the whole law is summed up in one sentence:
"Love your neighbor as yourself."

15 If you go around biting one another's heads off,
watch out or you'll be destroying one another
like cannibals.

16 What I mean is, let the Breath of Life guide your steps
and you won't be giving way
to self-destructive impulses of the flesh.

17 Mere flesh desires things contrary to the Breath of Life,
and the Spirit is against mere flesh for its own sake.
These two tendencies are at war with each other,
so it's no wonder you can't do everything you want.

18 But if you are led by the Breath of Life,
you won't be law-ridden.

19 The actions that mere flesh leads to
are easy enough to spot—
fornication, dirty-mindedness, immodesty, lazy softness,

20 worshipping idols, witchcraft, feuds, arguments,
scheming ambition, temper tantrums,
bickering and divisiveness, factions,

21 jealousy, murder, drunkenness, orgies,
and so on down the list.
I can tell you now as I have said before,
people who do this kind of thing
are not going to make it to the kingdom of God.

22 But the good effect of the Breath of Life is:
love, joy, peace, patience, kindness, generosity,

23 long-suffering, graciousness, fidelity, modesty,
self-control, purity.
There is no law against things like this.

24 Those who belong to Christ
have crucified their body's vices and wild desires.

25 If we live by the Breath of Life,
let us walk where this Spirit leads us.

81

Gradual cultural changes in Christian expression

For forty years the Judaism of Jerusalem was the strongest single cultural influence upon Christianity. Definite differences in doctrine and a particular memorial celebration distinguished the Jewish Christians from Hebrews, but by and large early Christianity was Jewish in its cultural expression. Although the Jewish influence was to remain strong for perhaps another fifty years, its pressure upon Christianity was slowly waning and by the end of the first century it was evident that Christians were more distinctively Christian than they were Jewish.

There were three reasons for the lessening influence of Palestinian Judaism in Christian circles. The first was the increasing number of Gentile converts who had no Jewish cultural background. The second was the total destruction of Jerusalem about 70 A.D. by the Romans, who were fed up with the nearly constant guerilla warfare of certain Jewish patriots.* The third was the growing formalization of what constituted the Jewish way of life which was defined by the Jewish leaders after the destruction of Jerusalem in order to preserve the heritage once symbolized by the Temple. It was this form of Judaism which the later gospel writers wrote about and against. Between the two (Jewish Christianity and rabbinical Judaism) there was continuous and open disagreement. It was this fact, together with the Pauline doctrine of salvation in Christ and not in the Torah and the admittance of Gentiles to the company of Christians, which led to a complete split and the formation of a separate Christian Church, whose leaders were not Jews in the strict sense, but Christians.

After the destruction of Jerusalem, Christian leadership came more and more from places like Antioch in Syria, a Roman town about 300 miles north of Jerusalem, Alexandria in Egypt, and the Greek cities where St. Paul had preached. Each of these cultural centers added its own influence to the self-understanding of the Church, and as they were slowly becoming more and more Christian, Christianity was becoming more and more universal. Up to this time Christian thought had been expressed in the

---

* For an interesting and rather detailed account of the long struggle, see Max I. Dimont's *Jews, God and History,* p. 101f.

thought forms of the Judaism of Jesus' time; after this, Christian thought began to take on the special characteristics of the languages formed by the cultures of Asia Minor, Egypt, Greece and North Africa. What effect this was to have on Christianity we shall see at a later date.

As Christianity spread and came into contact with other cultural forms, it encountered a challenge totally different from any it had met before. *This was the challenge of theology.* Although the theological conflict resulted in better understanding of the meaning of Christ and a clearer presentation of Christian belief, it was by far the most serious threat Christianity had encountered. The challenge was in the arena of thought. Here was the real test of Christianity's soundness.

For nearly two hundred years before the coming of Jesus religions in the Roman empire were becoming less and less distinct from each other. As people began to meet other people through trade and conquest, religions tended to fuse together. This tendency (best illustrated by the inclusion of several national gods in the famous Mt. Olympus* in Greece and the tolerance of Rome toward all religions) known as *Syncretism*** was a real challenge for primitive Christianity because it "stood for" much the same things as Christianity: tolerance, goodness, high moral tone—all of the classical appeals of philosophical humanism.

In its most challenging form it appeared under the title of *Gnosticism.* Gnosticism claimed to be a sure way to the knowledge, hence the vision, of God. It claimed that its rites, ceremonies, prescriptions and its "way" to God were divinely inspired and were transmitted to the elite (the in-group) through a mysterious tradition. It claimed that its magical rites and philosophical formulas offered an infallible means to salvation.

Gnosticism appealed to the educated and sophisticated in the same areas where Christianity began to have an influence. Because the Gnostics could see the good in Christianity, they were convinced that Christianity was just another form of Gnosticism and they interpreted Christianity as such. For the Gnostics knowledge was the key to the divine secrets. Because they considered matter to be essentially evil and Jesus was a material

---

* See *The Religions of Man,* "Three Ancient Religions."
** The harmonizing of, or union of, conflicting religious beliefs.

man, he could not be Messianic, for God would not use evil matter to secure a good end. It was obvious, then, that not Jesus but knowledge—pure thought—was the real savior of men. Their arguments were very profound and very persuasive.

Christianity survived this challenge because Christians relied on the human experience of Jesus as presented in the preaching of the apostles and depicted in the Gospels. For the Christians, faith was in the Person of Jesus, not in knowledge, philosophical speculation, or in magical practices which were supposed to have some secret saving power.

This theological problem faced by the early Christian community highlights a challenge constantly faced by those who propose a particular answer to the mystery of life. The discoveries of each age require a new understanding of the explanation proposed by any religion. As soon as Christianity moved away from its Jewish surroundings, it came face to face with other thought systems; it therefore faced the challenge of new explanations. To recount all of the challenges faced by the early Christians would require a book of its own. It should be obvious that the Christian Church faces a constant challenge to recast its thought forms for people of new cultures and new times. It must not only face different civilizations and different world views; it must cope with new languages, new concepts, new socio-economic forces. *But always its message and mission are the same: to bring the meaning of Christ as it has received it from the apostles to every people in every age.*

The end of the first era

By the close of the first century, Christianity had spread to all the territory of Rome. It had, in reality, become a "universal" church. A phenomenon of the time was the importance all Christian communities placed on the "Roman" Church.

From the time of St. Peter's coming to Rome and St. Paul's imprisonment in Rome the rest of the Churches looked to Peter, then to the Roman bishop, the successor to Peter, for guidance in doctrinal matters. The bishop of Rome was always asked for his opinion in ecclesiastical disputes. This was due, not to the fact that Rome at that time was the seat of the Imperial Roman Government, but to the special role St. Peter played in the formation of the apostles. The other apostles had established Christian centers elsewhere just as Peter had done, but only Peter was considered "first" among equals, whether in Jerusalem, Antioch or Rome.

As the center of Christianity moved from Jerusalem to Antioch to Alexandria and finally to Rome, its own self-understanding began to emerge. Its struggles for self-identity, its understanding of its mission, its theology and its structure developed and began to assume patterns which were to remain for centuries.

Christians gradually came to realize that they were not simply a Jewish sect (they viewed Judaism, finally, as transitional, for the Messiah had come). They also understood that the commission Jesus gave to his apostles was meant for all mankind, that Jesus' vision of man was real and pursuable, and that his future-oriented ideals were meant for this world because the Church is a concrete reality always dealing with the here and now.

Christian theology developed to elaborate the basic conviction that Jesus was divine, that he rose from the dead to bring his new life to all mankind, and that he was alive and active in his followers through his Spirit. From these beliefs arose the structure of the Church: bishops as successors to the apostles, priests as ministers of God's word and sacrament to assist the bishops, and the entire Church as the New People of God.

The first phase of the Church's thrust in the world developed over some one hundred years. Its second phase—understanding its relationship to the state—was to take place in the next era. Christians were to learn, through persecution, bitter experience and a large scale set-back that the kingdom of God announced by Jesus was not primarily a political kingdom, even though politics played a large role in its struggle, was not attached to armies or wealth or prestige or power. It was a hard lesson to learn, but it was worth it, for the Church moved steadily forward in its self-understanding and in its role in the world. With amazing swiftness, and in spite of overwhelming

85

odds, it grew from a small group of disciples into a mass of believers spread throughout the Mediterranean basin.

Christians believe that the "miraculous" spread was due to the Holy Spirit, for it seemingly could not be explained by human means alone. And besides, their belief in a saving God necessitated belief in His action in the world. How else did God work except *through* people whom He guided by the Spirit?

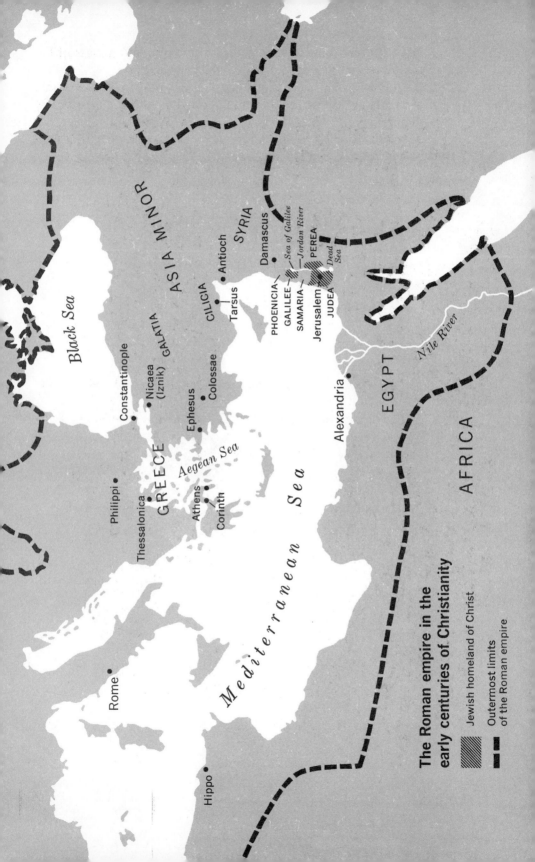

The Roman empire in the
early centuries of Christianity

Jewish homeland of Christ

Outermost limits
of the Roman empire

ASIA MINOR

GALATIA

CILICIA

SYRIA

Black Sea

Constantinople

Nicaea
(Iznik)

Antioch

Tarsus

Damascus

Sea of Galilee

Jordan River

PEREA

Dead
Sea

PHOENICIA

GALILEE

SAMARIA

Jerusalem

JUDEA

Ephesus

Colossae

GREECE

Aegean Sea

Nile River

Alexandria

EGYPT

AFRICA

Philippi

Thessalonica

Athens

Corinth

Mediterranean Sea

Rome

Hippo

Christianity established

Christianity appeared on the world scene at a very opportune time, for the initial growth of Christianity was directly related to the political fortunes of the Roman Empire.

By the time Jesus was born (during the reign of the great Augustus, 27 B.C.-14 A.D.) peace had reigned for 25 years in the territory controlled by Rome. There had been uprisings in various sections of the Empire, but, by and large, the entire Mediterranean basin was a rather nice place to live. Crime was at an all-time low, pirates were swept from the seas, and bandits led a precarious existence. Two important features of the Roman civilization which helped the spread of Christianity were the Roman roads and the Greek language. The one was a central factor in the economic prosperity of the empire; the other gave the advantage of a common language.

Christians interpreted the times as providential. If the Roman civilization had not been so advanced, it is probable that Christianity would have had a harder time spreading. In our eyes the times *were* providential; they contributed to the growth of Christianity, but also provided a new challenge: *What was the relationship of Christianity to world politics and world culture?* The response to this challenge gave Christianity a partial answer in its continued quest for self-understanding.

The growth of the Christian Church was closely associated with the political and cultural conditions of the time. The effect of this association shaped the doctrinal, liturgical and moral stance of the Church down to the present day.

The Roman World

What was this "Roman World" which affected the Christian Church so fundamentally that its basic forms and expressions remained well into the twentieth century?

It is simplest to say that it had two predominant strains; *the one, Roman, was political; the other, Greek, was cultural.* Rome was the predominant political power and ruled the Mediterranean world. Greece was the center of culture and had been so for over six hundred years, even though its empire had been conquered nearly three hundred years before by the Romans.

Greek culture has been the inspiration of Western man and the greatest force in the development of mankind the world has ever seen. In practically every aspect of human life the Greeks have led the way or at least laid the foundation for the achievements of Western culture. The ancient Greeks from the seventh century before Christ through the fourth century after Christ were outstanding in the fields of art and architecture, poetry and history, statesmanship and law, literature and rhetoric, science and philosophy.

Perhaps the greatest legacy of the Greeks, however—and surely the inspiration for all their great achievements—was their belief that man must be respected for his own sake as a free creature. "The world is full of wonderful things," wrote the Greek dramatist Sophocles (496-406 B.C.), "but nothing is more wonderful than man." This concept was the basis for their philosophy, their system of government, their art and architecture, and even for their representations of their gods.

The most important influence the Greeks have exerted over the centuries is in the field of thought. Because they had great respect for man, they paid greatest attention to those things which would enable every man to lead what they considered the good life; hence, their constant attention to all fields of learning. They had great schools and great teachers and encouraged all their bright young men to search for truth wherever it led. It is amazing how profound they were and how basic in spite of the limited resources at hand. In the field of thought they are most noted for their philosophy (the search for wisdom), as represented by their two great philosophers Plato (429-347 B.C.) and Aristotle (384-322 B.C.), who have had a greater influence on Western men's minds than any other thinkers. Both had a profound effect upon Christianity because their thought systems were the medium used to express Christianity in the crucial period after the first hundred years.

The Greek way of life was admired by every culture in the Mediterranean world and affected every culture to a greater or lesser degree depending on their sphere of influence.* None admired the Greeks more—or envied them more—than the Romans.

The Roman armies brought Greece under the rule of the Roman government about 200 B.C. By comparison with the Greeks, the Romans were a barbarous, uncivilized people; in fact, the Greeks despised their Roman conquerors, and their cool, detached attitude toward the Romans not only humiliated the Romans, but infuriated them. In an effort to imitate the Greeks and to learn from them, the Romans brought many Greeks to Rome as slaves to be their teachers. The program was successful, for Roman art, literature and philosophy flourished only after Rome had conquered the Greeks. Roman achievements in these fields are almost a direct copy of the prevailing Greek modes. It was thus the influence of Greek culture upon Roman civilization that made Rome what it was except for one uniquely Roman contribution: the highly organized and efficient Roman system of government. By it the Romans controlled the entire Mediterranean world—the area including present Portugal, Spain, France, Southern England, Southeastern Germany, and all of the lands bordering on the Mediterranean in Europe and Africa and the Near East.

It was in this world that Christians lived once they had moved out of the Jerusalem area. As early as St. Paul's journeys in the first years after the death of Jesus, Christianity had begun

---

* Alexander the Great (356-323 B.C.) had brought Greek culture to every major country in the Middle East. This is the territory we refer to as "the Greek world."

to move into the Roman world, and as more and more non-Jews became Christians the influence of Greek thought upon the Christian message became greater and gradually modified Jewish modes of thought.

In the previous chapter we saw one effect of non-Jewish culture upon Christianity in the decisions made at the First Council in Jerusalem. We shall now explore further influences of non-Jewish culture on Christianity in its next two hundred years.

Christianity did not move into the Greco-Roman world in a vacuum. The people of Greece and Rome were familiar with the Hebrew way of life and the Hebrew Scriptures,* and admired the Hebrew religious orientation and ethical life. Many Greeks and Romans had become Jews, and almost every major city employed some Jews in high positions of government because of their intelligence and attention to work.

When the first Jewish Christians came to preach Jesus in the great cities of the Roman Empire, they found Jewish communities well established and flourishing. The message was preached first to the Jews, but many pagans were attracted as well. As more and more non-Jews became Christians, the Christian preaching began to reflect the Greek modes of thought. *It was not long before Greek thought replaced Jewish thought as the standard way of expressing the meaning of Jesus.*

The Greeks were highly speculative people. Their philosophical traditions had trained them to look into the nature of things, to analyze, to ask why, to go to the center of the thought. This created a major shift in the Christian doctrinal presentation. *In the Jewish phase of Christianity the emphasis had been upon the experience the apostles had had of Jesus. In this Greek phase, the emphasis was upon the philosophical and theological meaning of Jesus.* It is because of this shift that we see, in this second phase of Christianity, the rise of Christian theology and the beginnings of those doctrinal debates which were to give the Church profound new insights into the meaning of Jesus. These discussions, chiefly centering around the nature of Jesus as the Son of God, caused Christianity to begin to develop its dogmatic style of crystallizing its beliefs in precise creeds with a technical vocabulary.

---

* The Hebrew Scriptures had been translated into Greek nearly *two hundred years* before Christ.

The Christian Greek influence

It is important to remember that Christianity did not *replace* Greek culture—it *Christianized* it. By the time Christians began to have a substantial following in the Grecian spheres of influence, the face of Greek civilization had already begun to shift from what is known as the Classical Greek Period, to what we refer to as the Greco-Roman Period—a slow transformation that resulted from the interaction of these two major cultures.

Greek Christians continued the cultural traditions into which they were born, transforming the Greco-Roman life from paganism to Christianity over a long period of time. The principal influence that Christians had on the civilization of the time was in philosophy and ethical conduct. A great number of Greek scholars became Christians and, as we have noted, brought their Greek learning to bear on the Christian message.

The great teachers, preachers and scholars who became Christians, and by their influence Christianized Greek culture, are called the Greek Fathers of the Church. Those men, whose lives span the 300 years from about 150 A.D. to 450 A.D. combined holiness and learning to such an extent that their contributions to civilization remain unique in the history of culture.

During this period, sometimes referred to as the period of Christian intellectualism, there was an astonishing development of Christian thought. The Greek Fathers, trained to be scientifically scrupulous in their pursuit of any topic, began a systematic explanation of the mysteries of Christianity. The result was an explosion of Christian knowledge, a better understanding of the Mystery of Christ, and an almost complete change in culture from paganism to Christianity in the Eastern Roman Empire.

Typical of these great men, and one of the first, was Origen (185-254 A.D.).* Origen lived in Alexandria in Egypt at a time when strong religious and philosophical ideals were

---

* The most famous Greek Fathers are Sts. Athanasius (293-373), Basil (329-379), Gregory of Nyssa (335-395), and John Chrysostom (344-407). Origen, who fell into disfavor because of some of his later ideas, is considered here because he began the long tradition of intense scholarship and writing for which the Greek Church is now famous.

wrestling for first place among the intellectuals of the city. Sophisticated Greeks, learned Jews, and clever Gnostics chided Christians for having "an unreasoned and vulgar faith." Although it is true that there had been learned Christian teachers before Origen, none had really come to grips systematically with the problems that Christianity posed for highly educated people. Origen began the long tradition in the Christian Church which treats theology as a religious science, founded, of course, upon the Faith as presented in the Scriptures, but subjecting its meaning to the rigors of intellectual examination.

Origen was particularly suited for this job. He was extremely bright, enthusiastic and gifted with judgment and quick insight. By the time he was 18, Origen was the head of a school (he was forced to go to work because the family needed support when his father was martyred). Within a few years the Christian school Origen headed was as famous as any of the Greek, Jewish or Gnostic schools in Alexandria, and Origen was considered the leading intellectual in the East. He was a prodigious worker and turned his sharp mind to theology, philosophy, Scripture, morals, law and poetry. It was to Origen that the famous phrase "he lived like a Christian but thought like a Greek" best applied, for he was an intense and holy Christian completely dedicated to Christian scholarship. From his time, Christian theology and philosophy ranked with the theology and philosophy of the non-Christians, and in his followers it surpassed all of them.

The spread of Christian influence to the Roman West

Although the majority of Christians were living in the Eastern half of the Roman Empire, Christianity was steadily moving to the West. There is no doubt that Christianity was preached in the countries east of Syria, but we don't know for sure what happened there. Perhaps the reason that the Christian influence spread westward is that the real Greek world was west of Jerusalem and the problems of language and travel in the Greek world were minimal compared to the same problems in the areas east of Jerusalem. It was natural for Greek-speaking Christians to move into those areas with which they were familiar.

Christianity had been brought to some of the major cities of the Roman West as early as St. Paul. A strong Christian tradition tells us that both St. Peter and St. Paul were put to death in Rome in the persecution under Nero about 67 A.D. The story of Christianity's development in the West is fragmentary at best. About all we know is that by the end of the first century the Christians were able to say that their religion was "universal,"* and that by 107 A.D. the famous martyr, St. Ignatius, referred to the Christian Church as "Catholic" and most people knew what he meant and to whom he was referring.

Almost by accident—in an occasional reference to a meeting, in an argument about some aspect of Christian faith, in a record of some small presentation here or there—we discover Christian communities in Spain, Portugal, France, the Germanic territories on the rim of the northeastern Empire, and in Roman Africa. Most of the territory was still pagan, of course, but Christians wielded great influence in the cities where they lived in the Roman Empire of the West.

Why were the Christians so successful in such a short time in both the Eastern and Western segments of the Roman Empire? Two of the probable reasons might be:

1) on the intellectual level—the Christian message made much more sense to the sophisticated and educated parts of society than did the pagan and mystery cults and the humanistic philosophies that were popular at the time;

2) on the practical level—it appealed to the poor, the uneducated, the slaves and the common man because of its message of love and hope.

Christianity was "everyone's religion." Rich and poor, freeman and slave, men and women were all proclaimed equal. All were encouraged to share equally, and all participated in the Lord's Supper. There were to be no divisions, no classes, no places of honor:

---

* By this they meant, of course, the universe they knew: the Greco-Roman world.

2:1 My brothers,
don't try to pick and choose among people
along with faith in Jesus Christ the Lord of Glory.

2 For example, suppose a man comes into your assembly
wearing an upper-class suit and a gold ring,
and along with him comes in a poor man
in shabby clothes—

3 and you take a look at the well-dressed man
and say, "You take the good seat over here,"
but you tell the poor man,
"Look, you stand over there" or
"You can sit on the floor by my footstool."

4 Aren't you sitting in judgment over one another
and passing rash judgments at that?

8 But if you keep the law of the Kingdom,
according to Scripture,
"You shall love your neighbor as yourself,"
then you will do the right thing.

9 However, if you act like snobs,
you are sinning against this law.

14 My brothers, what good is it
if a man says he has faith
but doesn't put it to work?
Do you think his faith is going to save him?

15 If your brother and sister are without clothes
and they are going hungry every day

16 and one of you tells them,
"Cheer up.
Stay warm and well fed."
—but doesn't give them anything for the body,
what good is that?

17 So faith, if it is not put to work, is dead.

St. Paul's celebrated words to the Christians of Galatia were no empty phrase. They were the working principle for Christian communities:

3:27 Whoever is baptized into Christ
has put on Christ.

28 He is no longer labelled "Jew" or "Greek,"
"slave" or "free man,"
"male" or "female."
Now you are all one in Christ Jesus.

The effect among those who became Christians was felt almost immediately, for it changed the attitude and the actions of the rich and the educated toward the poor, and afforded the poor the things they needed the most: understanding, sympathy and the practical things of life: food, clothing and shelter. There was a noticeable difference between Christian and pagan communities in the way the poor were treated.

Roman persecutions

Christianity's success, however, produced its severest trial, for it ran head-on into the power of the Imperial Roman government. Almost as soon as it gained a foothold in the cities of the Empire, it ran into trouble because of what it preached and what it stood for. It was not simply because it was a religion that Christianity suffered persecution from various Roman rulers (the Romans were the most tolerant of all people at that time), but because Christianity, unlike many religions the Roman government encountered, required involvement in man's earthly life. For Christians, religion was not an "extra-natural" segment of life. It was for real. It required a radical change in thinking and acting. For pagans, on the other hand, religion did not deal with their real lives; it dealt with a spirit world, with a "reality" that was only remotely connected with human life, with gods that had to be honored, appeased, or compensated for by rites and ceremonies that had very little to do with the business of living.

It must be understood, however, that most people in pre-Christian Greece and Rome were very religious. Every city and state had its own special gods whom all citizens were expected to worship in countless ways both public and private. In doing so, they not only performed a spiritual act, but demonstrated their loyalty to their city. Atheism was regarded as a crime against the state as well as against the gods, and an atheist (that is, one who denied the gods of the city or the state) might be executed or exiled.

When Rome conquered the people of the Mediterranean basin, it allowed them to continue their previous religious practices. Rome's attitude was one of toleration. But it did insist on one thing: to help unify all its different subjects and to insure their loyalty to Rome, it insisted that they add an extra god to their own group. Either this was a goddess called Roma to represent the Roman state, or it was the emperor himself. This action indicated loyalty to Rome. For the monotheistic Christians, however, compliance with this demand was impossible; thus, they came to be considered as traitors or as disloyal subversives who threatened their country's safety. This is the chief reason why Rome persecuted the Christians.

Another reason was the mystery that surrounded early Christianity, especially in its liturgical practices. Because non-Christians were excluded from the liturgy, the Church was thought of as a secret society. All kinds of rumors were circulated about the Christians, and the Roman people came to believe that Christians practiced evil and inhuman rites which no decent society could condone. Besides, when a man became a Christian, he often had to change his personal life, giving up former friends because they were pagans, or staying away from the immoral or blood-thirsty theaters and circus games. This made Christians unpopular; people called them "enemies of the human race." Minority groups always suffer from prejudice and discrimination because their style of life sets them off from their suspicious, often ignorant neighbors. As such a minority group, suspected of vile crimes and treasonable tendencies, the Christians lived in a hostile environment, which sometimes employed physical violence against them.

The Roman persecutions lasted for about two and a half centuries. They did not continue steadily throughout this period, however, and for many decades and in most places Christians lived in relative peace and security. The usually tolerant Roman government was reluctant to use force and in most cases avoided any open or systematic attempt to search out and persecute the Christians. However, in this case, as in so many other cases involving political motivation, everything depended on the circumstances.

100

For example, it was an accident that the first real persecution began in 64 A.D. Emperor Nero was blamed by his people for a great fire that destroyed much of the city of Rome. Knowing how unpopular the Christians were, and that the people would believe almost anything about them, Nero insisted that it was they who had started the fire. He arrested and executed several dozen Christians in the city, including St. Peter and St. Paul. "Their executions became sports events," wrote Tacitus, a Roman historian. "They were covered with wild animal skins and torn apart by dogs." But Nero did not order an attack on Christians outside of Rome itself, and the persecution soon ended.

Until about 250 A.D. the persecutions were sporadic and haphazard. But then a series of reforming emperors, Decius (249-251), Valerian (253-260), and Diocletian (284-305), anxious to strengthen the decaying empire, initiated three general persecutions designed to wipe out Christianity completely. These emperors regarded the Christians as a dangerous, disloyal group. In Egypt, Syria, and Asia Minor the government executed Christians, sent them to prison, enslaved them, and confiscated their property.

"The blood of martyrs is the seed of Christians," one of the early Christians wrote, for the persecutions failed to halt the Church's growth. Impressed by the Christians' piety and courage and by their loyalty to their beliefs, more converts joined all the time. Besides, their fellow citizens now realized that the Christians were not really a threat to the Roman way of life, for the Christians showed that they were quite willing to accept most of the great cultural and political achievements of the Greek and Roman people. In other words, because the People of God demonstrated that their secular culture did not have to be rejected when they professed belief in Christ, opposition to them died down.

In 313 A.D. Emperor Constantine issued the Edict of Milan, which cancelled all anti-Christian laws and granted complete toleration to the Christians. (By now, they made up about ten per cent of the Empire's population.) Constantine himself became the first Christian Emperor, and all following emperors except Julian (360-363) also took up the Christian faith. At the end of the fourth century, Emperor Theodosius (378-395) proclaimed Christianity the only legal religion within the Empire.

Not everything was a bed of roses, of course. There were selfish and cruel people who called themselves Christian—who had become Christians for one unworthy reason or another—and there were lying and cheating and adultery. The important thing, however, is that the conditions for the improvement of society were present. Slowly paganism began to disappear from the Western half of the Empire and by the end of the fourth century (approximately 400 A.D.) to be a Roman and to be a Christian were for all practical purposes identical.

Because the Roman West represented law and order, and because most of those who eventually became Christian leaders were "Roman thinking," they organized the Western Churches along the lines of the Roman Imperial government. The Christian Churches of the West were somewhat more highly organized than those in the East, and although the bishop of Rome was a bishop like every other bishop, he had more prestige because of his position than did the others and he was the virtual leader of the West regardless of his ability or his learning. He was called upon so often to settle both doctrinal and jurisdictional problems—because it was felt that he best represented the "apostolic tradition"—that he began to be looked upon as unique in his position. So great did his influence become that, when St. Augustine was bishop in North Africa (396 A.D.), he would write: "Rome has spoken, the matter is settled."

Doctrinal understanding develops out of the Christian East

As the Church grew in numbers and prestige in the Roman Empire, so did her understanding of herself and her mission. As the message of Jesus reached new cultures and transformed them, the preaching of the message and the understanding of the meaning of Jesus for the world developed.

As we have seen, it was obvious to the great teachers and preachers that the role of Jesus as Messiah had a much different meaning and application to non-Jews than it did to Jews. St. Paul recognized this early in his own ministry; and in every succeeding age, the church has had to face the challenge of this fact.

After the question of how Christians were related to Jews had been settled, the next doctrinal discussion centered around the Person of Jesus.

At this early stage of its development, the political center of Christianity was Rome, but the cultural center of Christianity was in the Mediterranean East and its leaders were Greek-speaking and Greek-educated. It was natural, therefore, that in the schools where Christians were teaching, the chief question asked was a theoretical one: "How is Jesus related to God?" The answers which various Christian scholars proposed to this question, created "schools of theology" in the major cities of the Eastern Roman Empire. As time went on, these schools of theology tended to polarize the answers to the question, and major differences arose which had an effect not only on the Church's understanding of Jesus and her formulations of her faith, but also upon the political scene at the time and for the next several hundred years.

It is impossible to understand this effect unless you understand the political and cultural developments taking place at the same time. During the last three-quarters of the fourth century, the Emperors took the Church under their protection, granted it concessions, and began to enact laws reflecting Christian principles. Because the Roman Emperor had been the supreme head of the pagan religion, he naturally felt that he had supreme power over Christian affairs also. Some of the Emperors acted as if they were bishops, even though they were not consecrated. This assumption of power created many problems for the Church. While the Emperors helped win converts and donated much wealth to the bishops, their interference in the doctrinal affairs of the Church complicated things immensely.

As we have said, Rome was the undisputed ruler of the entire Mediterranean world. It reached the peak of its territorial expansion during the reign of Trajan (98-117 A.D.). Because the territory was so vast, changes in governmental administration were necessary. When there were strong Emperors, the territory could be ruled by one man; when there were lesser men, the territory on the rim of the Empire required strong local rulers to keep it in tow. Eventually two major centers of government were established, one in Rome, the other in Constantinople about 1000 miles to the east on the straits between the Aegean and the Black Seas. By the end of the century (395 A.D.), the Empire was permanently divided with an Emperor in the East and an Emperor in the West. Culturally, the East and the West were poles apart. This difference was to have a great effect upon the emerging Church—such an effect, in fact, that the Christian Church would eventually split into two different expressions of Christianity: the Roman Catholic Church and the Greek Orthodox Church.

The Greeks were a more thoughtful, inquisitive people than the Romans. They had a natural talent for rational analysis, and were always asking questions about the meaning of life, the nature of man, truth, goodness, justice and so on. They produced some of the world's greatest thinkers in literature, political science, philosophy, physics and mathematics. One historian has put it simply by saying that the Greeks taught mankind how to think.

The Roman people, on the other hand, could not create fine theories and rational interpretations, but they could get things done. Their talents were practical: engineering, building great highways, organizing armies and winning wars, and forming laws for the government of a world-wide empire. When the Romans conquered the East, they united in their single state and under one citizenship both kinds of talents; the speculative skill of the Greeks and the practical ability of the Romans complemented each other neatly.

These natural differences between the Latins and the Greeks were reflected in their Christianity. And remember that great cities like Alexandria in Egypt, Antioch in Syria, and later Constantinople were as much Greek centers as were Athens and Corinth. The Greeks approached Christianity as if it were a system of philosophy. They wanted to think about their beliefs. They tried to understand them as thoroughly as possible. They received from the missioners the traditional fundamentals of Christianity, and then they turned their trained minds on these beliefs in order to understand them better. They believed that Christ was both God and man, for example, but they wanted to know exactly what this meant. They accepted the idea of the Trinity, but they tried to understand how the three divine Persons of the Trinity could be one God. In other words, the Greeks represented the Church's search for self-understanding.

In trying to use their minds to comprehend as much as possible of their faith, they created the science of theology.

Important Greek Christian thinkers became fascinated with particular parts of the Church's teaching. They asked themselves questions, and they asked other Christians too. Debates were held. Books were written. Different explanations were suggested. Lively discussions raged everywhere as evidence of the vitality of the Faith among these intense searchers for truth.

This sort of thing was not new. We have already seen that the Christians discovered that they were not a Jewish sect and that they were not Gnostics. They were now discovering that they were not a state religion. This attempt at self-understanding is a process that goes on all the time within the Church, either on the part of individual Christians or on the part of the entire tribes or nations which contemplate accepting Christianity. Through this process Christianity becomes meaningful to different men and to different times. By their discussions the Greeks came to understand the meaning of the Faith, and at the same time they contributed immeasurably to the total growth of Christianity, for all Christians since then have benefited from their probing and questioning.

While the Greeks were probing the depths of the gospel message, the Roman influence on the Christian Church became evident in its organizational structure. The Christians accommodated the Church's organization to the already existing political subdivisions of the Empire. Every major city became the headquarters of a bishop, who was the chief administrator of the Church. Some of the greatest cities such as Rome, Constantinople, Alexandria, and Antioch, were governed by bishops with the honorary title of patriarch. This meant that he supervised a number of bishoprics in his area. St. Peter had gone to the capital of the Empire, Rome itself, and thus his successors as the Church's chief leaders came to live in Rome. The title "papa" or "pope" was originally used for all bishops, but eventually it came to be limited to the bishop of Rome.

Although the bishop of Rome was generally recognized as the Church's supreme authority on earth, the great distances and the poor means of communication in those days left much of the actual business of the Church in the hands of the scattered bishops. When questions of the meaning of the Faith arose, people turned to the bishops for guidance. The bishops met together at different

105

times to consider such questions as were raised by the Greek thinkers. These meetings were called "councils." Councils became very numerous during the fourth century. The more important or difficult the questions, the larger the councils became as more and more bishops were brought into the discussions. Since most of the great theological debates occurred in the East, it was there that most councils met.

The debates on the nature of Christ serve as a classic example of how the Church arrives at an understanding of itself. The formulas of explanation indicate the Church's thinking at a particular time and in a particular place. As in any human attempt at meaningful explanation (for example, in Einstein's theory of relativity), there is an experience of a situation or an awareness of a reality, then there is an examination and a discussion of the reality, finally there is a theoretical expression of the experience as it is understood at the time. The resulting formulation into a theory then conforms to what some thinkers today call "the law of complementarity": the theory is held in a kind of suspension, accepted as the best explanation until a better explanation can be arrived at through clearer understanding of more data. The same process is followed when the matters under consideration are religious.* The debates on the nature of Christ held in the second half of the first 500 years followed this pattern.

For over one hundred years the Eastern Church had had running debates on the nature of Christ and the meaning of the traditionally accepted conclusions about the Trinity. These debates were carried on by sincere, zealous and learned men. They were searching for meaning; they were reacting to what they considered false or misleading interpretations of the meaning of Christ. In almost every school of thought, the basic idea was formulated and fostered by a single person of very persuasive character. When the debates got serious, that is when factions arose on either side of the argument and differences created violence, meetings were held by local bishops to determine whether or not this or that idea was in keeping with the traditional understanding of the Church. The history of this time is filled with

---

* For example, the Church's new insights about its role and mission in the twentieth century resulted in the discussions and documents of Vatican Council II.

examples of meetings of bishops in a particular area to discuss one or another of the proposals presented by the major schools of theology in Egypt, Syria, Palestine and Greece.

Once Christianity ceased to be a religion in hiding and came under imperial protection, the debates were no longer local; they were the concern of the whole Church. Because the Emperor took it upon himself to enter the discussion, the debates assumed a political dimension as well.

These expanded debates on the nature of Christ arose at the end of a severe period of persecution. They were brought to a head by a brilliant and persuasive Eastern priest, Arius (?260-336 A.D.), who, overwhelmed by the majesty and grandeur of God, preached that Jesus was not the Son of God (in the traditional Catholic sense), but was a man with certain divine characteristics and attributes. He argued that, if God was not material, he could not show himself humanly; therefore, Jesus was not God.* If this was so, then mankind was not really redeemed. This teaching was contrary to the entire Christian tradition, but, because Arius was so forceful and persuasive, he had a great following. Many powerful men, both churchmen and political leaders, defended him. Arius was no dummy, and he did not just put out ideas to create a sensation. He firmly believed that God was so completely outside of the created world that he could not possibly enter the world. (At this time, you will recall, most people believed in the heavens as a place for the gods, the earth as a place for man, and the underworld as a place for the dead.) Arius said, therefore, that Jesus could be no more than God's highest creature.

Arius' ideas created such controversy in the East that physical violence developed. Emperor Constantine decided to call a General Council of the Christian bishops to settle the issue. The Council met in May 325 A.D. in a small town near Constantinople, Nicaea (present day Iznik).

It is impossible to recreate the emotional atmosphere of this occasion. For the first time since the apostles met in Jerusalem in 49 A.D., bishops from all over the Christian world assembled. For the first time bishops were able to meet together under the sponsorship of an Emperor who personally endorsed Christianity.

---

* This was similar to the old Gnostic argument discussed on page 83.

It was inevitable that Constantine would dominate the Council, not by his theology, of course, but by the force of his person and position.*

Bishops from Egypt, Syria, Palestine, north Africa, modern Turkey, Persia, Greece, Italy and Spain, gathered together—men as diverse as the races and cultures from which they came. They were divided, not only by Eastern and Western modes of thought, but also according to what they understood of Arius' doctrinal expressions. What information we have tells us that 318 bishops assembled at Constantine's invitation together with experts in all fields, and priests, laymen, soldiers, and dignitaries from all professions and vocations.

Among the bishops on both sides of the issue under discussion—and adding drama to the whole scene—were men who had suffered persecution (the highest mark of honor among Christians) because they were Christian. There were bishops who had been branded with hot irons, men whose bodies bore visible scars of horrible torture, of scourging, mutilation, stretching on the wrack, men whose eyes had been gouged out, whose hands had been cut off, and men who had been galley slaves for years. There were intellectual giants, astute and crude politicians, parish priests, hermits and monks. There were powerful bishops from large dioceses and bishops from unknown towns. But they all came with one purpose in mind: to preserve what they understood as the message of Christ. They might respect the Emperor but they did not fear him. They might use politics to help their cause, but there was no doubt in their minds as to why they had assem-

---

* It is difficult for us in the twentieth century to understand the absolute power of the Roman Emperor. He was supreme in every detail of life. He had full legislative power, was the final judge in lawsuits, controlled currency, economics and politics, and dictated the religion that was to be practiced by his subjects. He was "emperor" because he was commander-in-chief of the armies (emperor comes from the Latin *imperator* which means "commander"); and he maintained his power and prestige as long as he controlled the army. Constantine, whose father had been "sub-emperor" in the West, succeeded to the throne because he controlled all the armies in what is now Portugal, Spain, France, Belgium and the southern half of England. From this power base he defeated the Emperor of the East, and thus controlled the entire Roman world. His word was absolute law; he controlled the destiny of every man, woman and child in the Empire. It was by his favor that any form of life was openly allowed; hence, the Christians, newly relieved from their persecutions and sensitive to the prestige of the Emperor, were anxious not to do anything that would upset the status of freedom they so lately acquired.

bled. This was a serious religious meeting. Its end and aim were religious.

When the Council finally opened, debates were held between those who believed that Arius was right and those who believed that his teaching destroyed the very meaning of Christianity. After a month's time the delegates were able to draft a formula which, they felt, expressed the traditional belief of Christianity. This formula, amended later to include items from later Councils, is the expression of faith that Catholics recite at Sunday Mass to the present day. At the present time, almost every Christian Church recites this formula or one nearly like it to express its beliefs. It is well to note that the Nicene Statement does not attempt to prove a fact but to formulate a Catholic belief. In its approved form in 325 A.D., it looked like this:

We believe in one God,
the Father almighty, Maker
[*of heaven and earth, and*]
of all things visible and invisible,
and in one Lord Jesus Christ,
the only-begotten Son of God,
Light of Light, true God of true God;
begotten not made; consubstantial with the Father,
by whom all things are made,
who for us men, and for our salvation,
came down [*from heaven,*] and was incarnate
[*by the Holy Ghost of the Virgin Mary*];
and was made man;
[*He was crucified also for us*],
suffered [*under Pontius Pilate, and was buried*].
The third day He rose again [*according to the Scriptures*];
and ascended into heaven
[*and sits at the right hand of the Father*];
and He shall come [*again with glory*]
to judge both the living and the dead
[*of whose kingdom there will be no end*].
And I believe in the Holy Ghost.

(The words in italics have been changed in some modern creeds to suit local conditions. The words in brackets were added to the original formula by later Councils, which also added certain statements to affirm a Christian belief.)

Once this "Nicene Creed" had been publicly signed by all the bishops and promulgated by Constantine, it became the official creed for all Christians. To deny the divinity of Christ in any way was to put oneself outside of the Christian community and was a crime against the state. However, the dispute did not end with the close of the Council. Powerful friends of Arius appealed to the Emperor, and some Eastern bishops withdrew their signatures. This dispute continued for several years and created other doctrinal discussions because various theologians and bishops, attempting to explain the meaning of the Nicene formulas, exaggerated now one aspect, now another. As a result, succeeding ages wrestled with such problems as the role of Mary, the nature of the Holy Spirit, and the meaning of salvation. As each discussion became heated, successive Councils were held (381, 431, 451 A.D.). At each the Nicene formula was re-affirmed and statements were added re-affirming the traditional Christian belief.*

Although Christian doctrinal formulations were born in the intellectual controversies of the time, and although the parry and thrust of these minds and the personality conflicts involved are of little concern for us today, what did come from these controversies is important, for they are the basic formulas in which we modern Christians have been taught the Mystery of Christ.** We believe *what* we do and we understand *as* we do because the intellectual giants of the first 500 years of the Christian era wrestled with the problem of the meaning of Christ.

---

* In Roman Catholic history there have been twenty-one General Councils, not counting the meeting of the Apostles in Jerusalem in 49 A.D. The first eight (from 325 to 870 A.D.) were dogmatic, that is, Councils which defined Christian doctrine to counter the heresies that cropped up about the meaning of Jesus. The eight Councils of the medieval period (1123 to 1417 A.D.) were largely political or reform Councils. The three Councils of the Renaissance Age (1439 to 1563 A.D.) were reforming Councils, whose purpose was to change the moral and religious tone of Christendom. The two Vatican Councils (1870 and 1965 A. D.) attempted to define the nature of the Church in a scientific age. (For a detailed and human account of the Councils, see Philip Hughes, *The Church in Crisis,* New York, Doubleday, Image Books, 1964.)

** The term "mystery," as in "Mystery of Christ" or "Mystery of the Church," means a divine reality inserted into history. The use of this term indicates that the reality cannot be fully explained or "captured" in human language.

Theology in the Western Church

Even though the cultural center of Christianity was located in the Eastern Empire, the Western half of Christendom was not without its centers of influence and learning. As far as we know, the intellectual center of Christianity in the West was located in Roman Africa, in cities along the northern coast of Africa which were already tied to Italy by commerce, culture and government.

Western schools of theology gave more attention to practical theology than did the Eastern schools. Western Christian scholars, schooled in the Roman tradition of practical government, put most of their efforts into changing men's lives and dealing with immediate problems of this world. A significant, though secondary factor in the difference between Eastern and Western theology was that from the time of Tertullian (about 160 A.D.) Western theology, for the most part, was written and preached in Latin and used Latin modes of thought to express its cultural ideas.

Tertullian, a lawyer, writer, and eloquent speaker, was the first of a long line of influential Western theologians who were to have a lasting effect on the philosophy and theology of the Western Church.

There were many great Christian teachers and preachers in the West. However, generally speaking, the period of the Western Fathers of the Church was about a century later than the period of the Eastern Fathers. Outstanding in the West were Sts. Ambrose (340-397), Jerome (340-420), Augustine (354-430), and two outstanding popes: Leo (pope from 440-461) and Gregory (pope from 590-604), whose leadership did much to shape the form of the papacy and make Western Christian doctrine the "official" doctrine of the Western Church. The greatest of the Western Fathers was St. Augustine.

Augustine was born in 354 A.D. in Northern Africa. His mother was a Christian, his father a pagan. He was a bright, impulsive, restless student and led a wild, unrestrained life for about twenty years. Dissatisfied with his life and with the small opportunities he found in Africa, he went to Rome where he was a teacher for about ten years.

Under the influence of St. Ambrose, the popular and schol-

Botticelli: "Head of St. Augustine"

arly bishop of Milan, Augustine turned his attention to the study of Scripture. The enlightened and practical advice of St. Ambrose finally brought Augustine into the Church, and he was baptized in April 387 A.D. when he was thirty-three years old.

Shortly thereafter, he returned to Africa and began his career as a writer. In 396 he became bishop of Hippo, a small diocese in Northern Africa about 300 miles to the east of Carthage. For the next thirty-four years, he produced the great books which were to make him one of the most influential men who has ever lived.

St. Augustine was a unique genius. He was an intellectual of unquestioned brilliance, a writer of extraordinary ability, a first-rate theologian, a top-notch administrator, a great humanist and solid saint. Volumes have been written about him, yet each author says that no words can adequately portray the man or his influence. Of Augustine, more than of any other single man, it can be said that his ideas and his life were the principal (some say the saving) inspiration in shaping Western civilization.

He was a prolific writer. We still have most of his writing, which includes 232 books, over 350 long sermons explaining the Faith, and 260 lengthy letters explaining his viewpoints on the Faith. Among his 93 major works like *On the Trinity, On Teaching Christian Doctrine, On the Faith and the Creed,* and commentaries on the epistles of St. Paul and the gospel of St. John, two acknowledged masterpieces remain on everybody's list of the greatest works ever written. The first, and still considered the greatest autobiography ever written, is his *Confessions,* his own story of God's saving action in his life. The second, *The City of God,* is Augustine's concept of the destiny of the world.

This last, the first "salvation history" book, is the work of a genius who could synthesize all of the aspects of history into a comprehensible whole. It is a philosophy of history, a theory of the state and of social life, and a summary of the complex relationships between spiritual and temporal authorities. At its center is the idea that Christ is the answer to the dilemma of human history, and the Church—the body of Christ—is the beacon light to guide civilizations in their self-expression. (Augustine's magnificent presentation of evil in society, and of its worst expression, war, is one of the very great passages on the existence of evil ever written.)

For thirty years Augustine was *the* voice of the Church in

the West. His influence grew to such proportions after his death that everything in Western Christendom—in theology, philosophy, culture and politics—was measured by its conformity with Augustine's ideas. His influence has been so great that the famous Protestant scholar Adolf von Harnack has said that "The inner, living piety found in Catholicism, and its expression, are essentially Augustinian." In the turbulent years that followed his death, in spite of the barbarian chaos and the theological upheavals in the Eastern Church, Augustine's theology and political philosophy shaped the theology and culture of the age.

This intellectual giant dominated Christian theology in the West for 800 years, until the time of St. Thomas Aquinas.*

The end of the second era

Once Constantine had officially granted religious freedom in the Roman Empire and succeeding Roman Emperors had taken an active part in the affairs of the Church, Christianity was finally established on firm ground. In the entire Roman Empire, it was no longer an outside sect, a religion practiced by a minority group. It was, unofficially at least, the religion of the Empire. The Mediterranean world was, to all intents and purposes, Christian.

By the same token, Christianity too had changed and developed. It had outgrown its Jewish beginning, had acquired an institutionalized form to function in society, and had developed a rather settled theological framework. It was, in the best sense, a religion for the world, for it preached in Greek and Roman concepts a Saving God who had entered man's world in the Person

---

* The influence of these two men on Western thought has been so great that the first "theological age" of Western Christendom might be called Augustinian, and the second Thomistic. You will note that a third Christian thinker, Teilhard de Chardin, assumes a similar position throughout these books for our own age. This is for several reasons: (1) We found his mode of thought was most apt for the development of our unifying theme as chosen. (2) He has greatly helped us in finding direction in the resolution of the science-theology dichotomy which we feel in us is an indication of the same developing conflicts in today's adolescents.

By giving him a position of such relative importance, we are not prejudging in an evaluation that can only be made by history.

of Jesus. It embraced people from every walk of life in every tribe and nation known to the Greco-Roman world, and its principles all but dominated the thought and actions of an entire empire.

Never before had a religion so captured the religious sense of so many people. Christianity had survived the opposition of Jewish religious leaders, the paganism of the Roman world, the disdain of the sophisticated, and the predictable odds against survival. But there was much to do. Even though the people of these times were only vaguely aware of the vast number of people who lived on the fringes of the Roman Empire, and though they were not at all aware of the cultures that flourished in India, China, Japan and the continent of Africa, and did not even dream of the existence of the Americas, the Church was conscious of its mission to all people and pushed ahead by sending missionaries to the known lands within the Roman orbit.

The Church was also conscious of its religious force within the world in which it operated. It knew that, even though it was deeply involved in the politics of the time, it was not a political party, a dependent group, a national or imperial religion. It knew that it should not pursue economic, political or cultural concerns primarily for their own sake, but for the sake of leading men through them to the divine. Christians knew that, though religion is a human way of expressing man's relationship with God and, as such, has economic, political and cultural interests, it is more than any of these alone and more than all three together. Christians knew that the meaning of Christ for their world went beyond the aims and purposes of human society and its institutions; it made mankind conscious of cooperating with a personal, Saving God.

As we look back into history to better understand our Faith, we can see the social and political progress of civilization. We can also see the development of its understanding in its ideas of God, the meaning of religion, and the expression of worship as well as in its ethical sense. Jesus did have an effect upon society: the greatest single force for change in the Western world was the entire Christian Church he founded.

Reading guide

Any student of history who is interested in depth-understanding of a particular period must research the era in terms of the people, events, related affairs, and the socio-economic and socio-religious concerns of the period.

The following book list is divided into two major parts. Part I lists books which will help you do research on topics covered in Chapters 1 to 4 of this book. Part II contains books which are particularly useful for Chapters 5 and 6. You will note that the list in Part II is divided into General History, Church History, and Historical and Biographical Novels. The novels are included because they give the "feel" of history, not simply the events. The particular novels listed were chosen because they emphasize the people and the culture that shaped the events of history.

You are urged to read at least one of the biographical novels or biographies in order to increase your understanding of the history that really shaped your life.

DAILY LIFE IN THE TIME OF JESUS
Henri Daniel-Rops, Hawthorne Press, New York, 1962

THE GOSPEL ACCORDING TO PEANUTS
R. L. Short, John Knox Press, Richmond, Virginia, 1965

HONEST TO GOD
J. A. T. Robinson, Westminster, Philadelphia, 1963

JESUS AND HIS TIMES
Henri Daniel-Rops, Hawthorne Press, New York

THE MYSTERY OF THE CHURCH
J. Powell, Bruce, Milwaukee, 1967

A NEW CATECHISM
Herder and Herder, New York, 1967

THE NEW TESTAMENT IN MODERN ENGLISH
J. B. Phillips, Macmillan, New York, 1960

THEOLOGY FOR BEGINNERS
F. Sheed, Sheed and Ward, New York, 1957

YOUR GOD IS TOO SMALL
J. B. Phillips, Macmillan, New York, 1956

A. *General History*

CLASSICAL GREECE
C. M. Bowra, Time Incorporated, New York, 1965

IDEAS AND INSTITUTIONS IN WESTERN CIVILIZATION
Norman F. Cantor (ed.), Macmillan Paperbacks, New York
    Volume 1: *The Ancient World* (to 300 A.D.)
    Volume 2: *The Medieval World* (300-1300 A.D.)

IMPERIAL ROME
Moses Hadas, Time Incorporated, New York, 1965

THE JEWS, GOD AND HISTORY
Max I. Dimont, The New American Library, New York, 1962

THE STORY OF CIVILIZATION
Will Durant, Simon and Schuster, New York, 1935-1968
    Volume 1: *Our Oriental Heritage*
    Volume 2: *The Life of Greece*
    Volume 3: *Caesar and Christ* (to 325 A.D.)

B. *Church History*

CHRISTIANITY THROUGH THE AGES
K. S. Latourette, Harper and Row, New York, 1965

HISTORY OF THE CHURCH
Thomas Neill and Raymond Schmandt, Bruce, Milwaukee, 1965

HISTORY OF THE CHURCH OF CHRIST
Henri Daniel-Rops, Image Books, Doubleday, Garden City, New York
      Volumes 1 and 2: *The Church of Apostles and Martyrs*
      Volumes 3 and 4: *The Church in the Dark Ages*

THE HORIZON HISTORY OF CHRISTIANITY
American Heritage Publishing Company, New York, 1964

ISRAEL AND THE ANCIENT WORLD
Henri Daniel-Rops, Image Books, Doubleday, New York, 1964

A POPULAR HISTORY OF THE CATHOLIC CHURCH
Philip Hughes, Macmillan Paperbacks, New York, 1962

RELIGION AND THE RISE OF WESTERN CULTURE
C. Dawson, Image Books, Doubleday, New York

THE WORLD'S GREAT RELIGIONS
Time Incorporated, New York, 1957

C. *Historical and Biographical Novels**

DEAR AND GLORIOUS PHYSICIAN   Taylor Caldwell
A re-creation of New Testament times with St. Luke as the
main character.

THE SILVER CHALICE   Thomas B. Costain
The magnificent story of a silversmith who was commis-
sioned to make a container for the Cup of Christ.

THE BIG FISHERMAN   Lloyd C. Douglas
The life of St. Peter is used to portray the real life of the
people in Arabia, Palestine and Rome.

THE ROBE   Lloyd C. Douglas
An imaginative story about what happened to the robe of
Christ. The whole pageantry of Jewish-Roman relations
comes to life.

THE GLADIATORS   Arthur Koestler
A story of Rome centering around the life story of Rome's
most famous gladiator, Spartacus, and the rebellion of the
gladiators.

THE SCARLET LILY   E. F. Murphy
A fictional portrayal of Mary Magdalene and the times of
Christ.

QUO VADIS   Henry Sienkiewicz
A great novel dealing with the Rome of Nero and the death
of St. Peter.

BEN HUR   Lew Wallace
The famous novel of Roman days in which Ben Hur escapes
from a life sentence as a galley slave and gets revenge on the
Roman friend who betrayed him.

---

* Arranged generally according to historical periods.

FABIOLA   Nicholas Wiseman
   A story of the Christian persecutions under Diocletian.

DARKNESS AT DAWN   Thomas B. Costain
   An historical romance set in the days of the barbarian
   invasions of the Roman Empire.

THE CONSCIENCE OF THE KING   Alfred Duggan
   A story of violence and intrigue in Britain of the fifth
   century.